Mediumship
Scrying &
Transfiguration
For Beginners

About the Author

Diana Palm (Stillwater, Minnesota) is a medium, author, and spiritual healer. She first learned how to heal spiritually by a priest in Medjugorje, Bosnia, in 1995. Diana studied mediumship at the world renowned Arthur Findlay College in England and is certified through the THInK Institute as a ThetaHealing® Instructor. Through a series of workshops, certification classes, and private sessions, Diana assists people with transforming their lives through healing. She speaks publicly about the afterlife and helps educate people spiritually so that they can live life in more meaningful ways as well as re-connect them to their loved ones in spirit. For upcoming events, visit her website at www.dianapalm.com.

Mediumship Scrying & Transfiguration

For Beginners

A Guide to Spirit Communication

Diana Palm

Llewellyn Publications
Woodbury, Minnesota

First Edition
First Printing, 2017

Cover design: Lisa Novak
Editing: Patti Frazee

ThetaHealing® is a registered trademark of ThInK Institute and creator Vianna Stibal

Llewellyn Publications is a registered trademark of Llewellyn Worldwide Ltd.

Library of Congress Cataloging-in-Publication Data
Names: Palm, Diana, author.
  Title: Mediumship scrying & transfiguration for beginners : a guide to spirit communication / Diana Palm.
  Other titles: Mediumship scrying and transfiguration for beginners
  Description: First edition. | Woodbury : Llewellyn Worldwide, Ltd., 2017. | Includes bibliographical references.
  Identifiers: LCCN 2017027386 (print) | LCCN 2017015178 (ebook) | ISBN 9780738752686 (ebook) | ISBN 9780738752488 (alk. paper)
  Subjects: LCSH: Crystal gazing. | Clairvoyance.
  Classification: LCC BF1335 (print) | LCC BF1335 .P35 2017 (ebook) | DDC 133.9/1—dc23
  LC record available at https://lccn.loc.gov/2017027386

Llewellyn Publications
A Division of Llewellyn Worldwide Ltd.
2143 Wooddale Drive
Woodbury, MN 55125-2989
www.llewellyn.com

Printed in the United States of America

Other Books by Diana Palm

Setting Spirits Free:
Clear Negative Energy & Help Ghosts Cross Over

Dedication

This book is dedicated to the mediums who commit their life to service, who hold the highest ethics in spirit communication, and who share their gifts through teaching others.

In loving memory of two of my mentors: Alan Arcieri and Rev. John Lilek.

contents

foreword

I first met Diana Palm in 2013 when she visited my house as part of an investigation conducted by the Minnesota Paranormal Investigators Group (MNPG). Diana's intuitive abilities and her skill at communicating with spirits were evident to me, and I was impressed with the professionalism of the entire MNPG crew. I appreciated the respect and courtesy with which they treated the spirits and my home.

Right from the start, I felt that Diana and I were kindred spirits. Like me, Diana lived in a haunted Victorian house in an historic river town, and, like me, she found living with spirits to be interesting and enjoyable.

As I recall, the MNPG crew was one of the first teams I hosted that took time during their investigation to check their EVP recordings so they could respond to anything the spirits said while they were still on site, thus engaging in highly interactive spirit communication during the investigation. This same practice of respectful and active engagement with spirits was also evident later that year when I attended a transfiguration séance with the medium Reverend John Lilek at Diana's beautiful home.

Even though I have long been intrigued by all facets of spiritualism, I had never heard of transfiguration séances. I *had* once seen the figure of (what appeared to be) an ancient African medicine man appear as a semitransparent image superimposed over noted anthropologist and author Michael Harner, PhD, when Dr. Harner was speaking at a shamanism conference I attended. I have also had the experience on several occasions of seeing my own face change while I practiced mirror scrying or mirror meditations. But an event in which a medium could intentionally call in spirits and be confident that the spirit faces would be visible to an audience for a full hour seemed pretty fantastic. The transfiguration séance at Diana's home delivered all that—and more.

Seated with the other guests in straight-back chairs in a clean and comfortable room in Diana's hundred-year-old basement, I tried to imagine who I might see that I knew from the spirit world. The air hummed with anticipation as Diana turned down the lights. Except for a dim red light shining directly on Reverend Lilek's face, the room was pitch-black. I felt my eyes straining to focus, and in no time, a dizzying succession of distinct, individual faces started to appear in place of Reverend Lilek's face. I saw the faces of men, women, and children. I saw Abraham Lincoln, my Grandpa Morgan and—very startling—a few alien-type faces. During the séance, Reverend Lilek's eyes were mostly closed, but in at least a couple of instances, the "eyes" of the spirit-world face were open and seemed to be looking around the room, which was eerie.

As the séance progressed, guests called out the names of people they recognized, including Abe Lincoln, which confirmed for me that others in the audience were seeing at least some of the same images I was seeing. Most moving to me, of course, was seeing my Grandpa Morgan's face. No one else recognized my grandpa, or at least, no one else called a name when his image appeared, which added to the credibility of the experience. As the session came to a close, the room was still buzzing with excitement.

When Diana asked me to write the foreword for her book, I immediately agreed. Diana is a natural teacher, knowledgeable and skilled, with a positive, empowering approach that illuminates and uplifts individuals on both sides of the veil. The fascinating true accounts in this guide illuminate our divine nature, and help us to understand what that means, both for our individual lives and for the evolution of humanity. I particularly admire Diana's philosophy of placing spirit world work in a practical context, teaching how to use spirit communication to increase respect, understanding, and compassion for other living beings in both the physical and spirit worlds.

—Annie Wilder, author of *House of Spirits and Whispers*, *Spirits Out of Time*, and *Trucker Ghost Stories*

introduction

Have you always wanted to see spirit but believed that the gift was only for a chosen few? Perhaps you have thought that if you could just see spirit for yourself, you would then be able to believe in the afterlife. How would this experience change your current belief system and how would it impact your spiritual perspective?

These are among the most common questions asked by those seeking to see spirit and I am happy to be part of this journey with you. The techniques offered in this book will empower you with the abilities that you seek so that you can formulate your own conclusions. I will also be sharing the least-known method of mediumship— scrying, which is designed specifically to help you develop your spiritual sight. This book will explain how to use the ancient art of scrying and transfiguration to open up your own spiritual sight and allow you to have your own interactions with the spirit world. I will share many methods of scrying, as all forms of scrying can help enhance your ability to perceive messages from the spirit world. By following the techniques presented in this book, you will be able to see spirits with your physical eyes.

I will explain how I came upon this knowledge through credible and gifted teachers, how it enhanced my own perception and abilities to see spirit, and how this same knowledge can help you to see spiritually too.

In my daily workings with the public, I have come across many people with an earnest, heartfelt desire to see spiritually. It may surprise you to know that many mediums do not actually see spirit with their physical eyes. If you are a medium and would like to enhance your ability to see spiritually, you will be delighted at how these simple techniques can help you do that. Having this ability can enhance the work you already do with spirit and may add another dimension to your spiritual gift.

However, these simple techniques are such effective tools that even normal everyday people can use them to gain spiritual sight. For those of you who find yourself contemplating the afterlife, wishing for one more glance at a lost loved one, or are merely curious; this book is for you too. Scrying and transfiguration can help you peer into the spiritual world, perhaps for the first time, as well as reconnect you with your loved ones.

I have found the greatest comfort in knowing that life continues after death, a belief that solidified for me with the knowledge gained through my own spiritual sight and personal experiences. While working in the field of paranormal research, I met countless people who sought to have spiritual interactions. This included paranormal investigators as well as the general public, who often experienced a spontaneous spirit visit or haunting. In fact, I found that most paranormal enthusiasts were people who had experienced firsthand something spiritual and wanted to learn more about the paranormal as a result.

Having a firsthand experience with a spirit often serves as a catalyst to wake you up spiritually. It's like opening a door that you cannot shut. Rather, once that door is open, it begins a deeper journey within, or a type of awakening process spiritually for the individual. This is often a time of contemplation when one challenges their current belief system and all that they have been taught in an attempt to merge their new perspective into their life.

For many people, this early phase of expansion can feel very intense. Family and friends may not understand it fully unless they, too, have had their own experience with spirit. You may even question if your interest in the spirit world has taken you over, almost like a drug, making you crave further experiences. Please, let me put all your fears to rest. This process, though it may seem intense at times, is absolutely normal. It is part of the growth process and is a natural part of the human experience.

If you have had a spontaneous experience with spirit, it perhaps occurred as an afterlife visit from a deceased loved one or a brief interlude with a ghost. Some people are naturally drawn to haunted locations and may live in a series of haunted houses as if their soul required the experience in order to wake up spiritually. I believe this was part of my soul's journey as it initiated me to the spirit world and helped to wake up my gifts of mediumship. Once you have seen spirit for yourself, it changes you forever. You will always feel the expansion of the experience within you and may spend the rest of your life seeking more spirit contact.

When the experience of seeing spiritually does not happen spontaneously, all that may be required is a heightened receptivity to spirit. This may be achieved through regular meditation practice, deep healing, and focused intentions. However, the scrying and transfiguration techniques presented in this book may provide an even quicker and easier way to access the spirit world at will.

Perhaps you are neither a medium nor a paranormal enthusiast, but nonetheless you desire to see spirit. This seems to be among the most common desires of mankind, permeating every culture throughout time. It is absolutely natural to ponder your existence in the vast universe and to wonder what happens after death.

Religions seem to have a variety of opinions about this experience and most acknowledge that there is a spirit world that follows physical death. Perhaps you have heard all the wonderful things about the afterlife but still reserve opinion due to lack of personal experience. You may be a seeker of truth and wish to experience the spirit world for yourself so that you can formulate your own opinions and ideas about it.

I have written this book for all of you. The skeptics, the believers, the mediums, the paranormal enthusiast, and the everyday person. It will take no special gift for you to follow the techniques described in this book to gain spiritual sight. I am excited to be able to share this information with you because I feel that it will help you become more aware of the spirit world that exists around us all and enable you to form your own opinions about it.

Over the last decade, I have taught countless people how to connect with the spirit world and increase their spiritual sight. I have found that most people will be able to do this immediately, and that it may take a little practice for others. However, I have never worked with anyone who just could not do it. You will be amazed at how easy it is and that these techniques will enable you to increase your abilities to see spirit very quickly.

It lights me up inside when I see a person react to seeing a spirit for the first time. I have worked with very gifted healers and mediums, paranormal investigators, ministers of different faiths, scholars, and nonbelievers. Everyone went into the process with an open mind and were exhilarated to discover that it really worked! I have had people cry tears of joy, fall out of their chairs laughing, and even become frozen and unable to express their delight. At last, a technique that works! If you are resonating with this feeling right now, you will really enjoy this book and all that scrying and transfiguration have to offer.

Keep in mind that this is a spiritual gift and should always be respected. Avoid the temptation to use this or any other spiritual ability for purposes of self-elevation. All our gifts are a divine inheritance but they can be taken away when improperly used. Always use your abilities for the highest good of all concerned and share it with love.

I am a medium, paranormal investigator, afterlife researcher, and ThetaHealing practitioner and instructor. In my previous book, *Setting Spirits Free: Clear Negative Energy and Help Ghosts Cross Over*, I share how to discern spirits, protect yourself spiritually, heal lost souls, and communicate with deceased loved ones. My training has also included attending mediumship classes at the world-renowned Arthur Findlay College in England. It is a school designated as the world's foremost college for the advancement of spiritualism and psychic sciences. It has been my personal preference to apply my training as a ThetaHealer to the many other disciplines of spirit communication I have learned. ThetaHealing is a meditation technique that is designed to slow down the brain waves into theta, which is a very receptive state of mind. Holding the intention to connect with Creator, it allows for a very high connection or increased vibration.

Due to the high vibrational nature of the technique, I find that it is easier for me to connect and access the spirit world. However, this book is written pure to the techniques of scrying and transfiguration as they were taught to me. If you feel led to use any other method or modality in combination with these techniques, it may serve to amplify your energy and quicken your abilities. There are many paths to working with spirit; you decide what works best for you.

—With love and gratitude, Diana Palm

Seeing Is Believing

A few short months after my little sister passed away, my husband and I decided to move our family to Florida. The loss of my sister had sent me into hours of quiet contemplation as I sought different methods of healing to work through my grief. It was her death (or perhaps her spirit's urging) that made me decide upon such a dramatic change in my life.

My sister had always shown support and fascination for the spiritual work I did. She held similar views toward healing, though her gift was aimed at working with animals.

The years preceding her passing, I had moved away from spiritual healing and held down an absolutely normal, mainstream job by owning my own home-staging business. But with the advent of her passing, I was drawn back into the world of spirit. Perhaps it was my self-imposed solitude that allowed my new receptivity of spirit. What had always remained along the fringes of my life opened up wide, becoming the main focus. The synchronicities in my life had multiplied along with an increase of supernatural or spirit activity.

As many of you may have already experienced, the loss of someone very close to you can change your life immeasurably. I chose to meditate, take classes for healing, and read spiritual books. I believe it was these actions that really helped to develop my spiritual gifts. I wanted to know more about what happened after physical death and was fascinated by the afterlife. The yearning to stay connected to my sister gave me the motivation that I needed.

This process of learning and opening up began to take its hold on me, as I no longer felt drawn to live my life the way I did before. The life I had created began to feel mundane as my passion for working with spirit sprang to the forefront. I resumed my normal occupation until I realized that the changes I had gone through impacted my career choice as well.

The precise moment came when I was teaching a large class on home staging. One of my students asked me if I was following my dream. She assumed that because I was so passionate about the topic of home staging that it must be my life path. I spontaneously answered that my true passion was actually for healing and connecting with spirit. The next moment was silent and as I looked inward, I realized that the change had occurred. Perhaps it solidified for me because I confessed it out loud to myself and the entire class.

Looking back, I can validate that this was one of my divine timings. We all have divine timings, which are moments in our life designed to put us on our soul path. You may have one divine timing or many. These are moments in life that change everything. They are strategically placed into your timeline as agreed upon before you decided to be born. Divine timings cannot be changed because they were set up by you.

As I spoke the words out loud to my class, they resonated so deeply with me that it was impossible to ignore or take back. Which, taken into consideration, meant that my life was about to change drastically. I didn't know how I would leap from the classroom and resolve my life as a home stager to step into the unknown—or even what that life would look like. But I knew that spirit was guiding me and that I would not be alone as I pursued my life path.

I relied heavily upon my faith as I intuitively followed the steps to make the necessary changes in my life. The guidance I received always arrived differently. Sometimes, it came through words spoken by strangers or friends. Sometimes, it arrived as an idea or inspiration from a dream. Other times, it came when I stumbled into a class that I later knew was meant for me. But one thing is for sure, once you have an epiphany like I did, you must follow through.

My family and I arrived in southwest Florida and began to familiarize ourselves with our new home, still open and watchful for spirit to guide our way. When you are being led by spirit, you will notice that unplanned things show up that often guide you to the right place or person. You can nurture more synchronicities in your life by following the ones that have already been sent to you. They are easier to recognize when you are in the energy of peace and expansion.

For me, on that day, it was the simple act of driving the convertible with the sun on my face. Moving from the cold Midwest, I was elated to be in the warm glow of sunshine and that was all it took. The sun (or enjoyment of it) ushered in a heightened state of awareness. As my husband and I turned the car onto what we thought was the wrong street, we noticed a large sign advertising a metaphysical healing center. Curiosity compelled us to pull over and check out the center.

We had no idea of the significance of the center or the people we would meet there, but I was thrilled to discover a place to purchase crystals, books, essential oils, and incense. The center offered many classes and psychic services, along with a wide variety of healing modalities. It immediately felt as if we had been led onto the back street of this very unfamiliar town for the sole purpose of discovering this center.

After inquiring about the classes offered, it was recommended that I sign up for a series of mediumship classes taught by Alan Arcieri. He had quite a large following of happy clients and students that held him in high regard. He had just written a book entitled *Earth School 101* and was a regular personality on local radio shows. I signed up for his classes right away and was excited to begin my adventure with mediumship.

Although I had seen and experienced ghosts and spirits spontaneously, I had never developed my abilities to do this on purpose. Frankly, I didn't know I could become a medium. I believed as others did—that mediums were born, not made. I also believed that a person had to come from a long line of mediums and that the skill could not be taught. I didn't know that I could develop this gift in order to help others connect with their loved ones, and I was excited to explore my potential.

Up until that moment, I was somewhat of a closet healer. I performed spiritual healings through a variety of techniques, but I did not advertise my services to the public. Perhaps I feared rejection from the mainstream or worried that I wasn't qualified enough. Close friends and colleagues had trusted me with their healings, which I mostly performed under the cover of night in private settings.

Many psychics, mediums, and spiritual healers spend the majority of their lives this way and it takes an act of courage to step beyond it. What helped me feel confident enough to work with the public was taking my training to a professional level by attending classes and earning certifications. I realized that like every other talent or skill, mediumship also required a lot of experience. It was as if this step in my development declared to the universe, and me, that I was ready to embrace my gift and learn how to use it. I believe that everybody has the ability and can also develop their gifts for mediumship.

Each class that Alan taught focused on a different aspect of opening our psychic and mediumistic abilities. Included were classes on meditation, psychometry, and energy healing. My abilities began to improve with regular weekly practice as I laid the groundwork for my future life's work.

The class that made the biggest impression on me was the one Alan taught on scrying. Scrying is a form of divination often used to predict future events or assist with clairvoyant abilities. It is associated with crystal balls, black onyx mirrors, clouds, or reading tea leaves. Scrying may be used to see into the past or to give clarity to a current life situation. I had read about scrying in its many different forms; however, Alan didn't have any tea leaves or magic mirrors. What he did have was my full attention when he stated that we were going to scry into our past lives. I didn't know that scrying could be used to see our past lives or that we could access this ability without any previous experience. I paid very close attention because I wanted to give this exercise my best effort.

The center was set up with small tables and sets of chairs dispersed throughout the room. The lights were dimmed and one candle sat upon each table. The students took their seats as Alan first guided us to protect our space. He told us to send energy to the third eye of our partner. We were told that if we held our concentration, we would be able to see through the veil and witness the faces of previous lifetimes of the person that we were gazing upon.

The room fell silent as we all began the process. I remember feeling worried that I wouldn't see anything and imagined that everyone else was more advanced than me. The hand on the clock passed and still the room remained silent. The exercise was slated to last twenty minutes and at about the sixteenth minute it finally happened; in an instant, my doubt dissolved as I began to see spirit faces emerge upon my partner. One after the next, they showed themselves in succession. Full and complete faces of men, women, children, and even an animal hybrid! I was elated that it worked and that I was able to see so many past life images. Each face that appeared was as real as if I were looking at a physical person sitting in front of me.

How was it that I had never learned this technique before? I am sure if I had known about it, I would have spent countless hours scrying with my siblings and teaching it to friends at sleepover parties. None of the metaphysical books I had ever read taught that scrying could be used in this way.

When the exercise was finished, we were all encouraged to share the images we saw with the entire class. For me, there was an unexpected impression that came through with each image. It was as if I saw how each previous version of the person had perished and I felt bits of their personality. I saw a young girl who was charred as if she was burned in a fire. I saw a woman whose lips were sewn closed with a thick black thread. There were many images of men and women with average-looking features, and then I saw a half human/half wolf.

As we went around the circle, no one mentioned seeing anything unhuman, so I wondered if I should share it with the group. The face was so distinct and so unexpected that I knew it was not my imagination; I reluctantly shared what I had seen. I described how the face of the woman I was partnered with began to shift. How her cheeks stretched outward and grew black patches of hair. How her nose flattened and turned into a shiny black muzzle. She had definitely taken on the form of a hairy half breed.

Alan was quick to note that we didn't all originate on planet earth and that it was entirely possible to run across ancient faces of non-human breeds that we have not seen before. That was a new concept for me and worthy of exploration.

If we didn't alltogether evolve from cavemen, where did we all come from? I began to research the topic until I found enough information to validate its premise. There were many ancient alien theories that suggested interplanetary crossbreeding. There were also the theories of star seeds being brought to earth from more enlightened planets. For centuries, ancient cultures from around the world have believed that humans originated on another planet. There were theories of interdimensional beings that had abilities to become physical when they intended to do so by adjusting their frequency and vibration, as well as visitors from multi-verses that coexist at the same time and space in an overlapping reality. I also found an interesting theory written about in *The Book of Knowledge, The Keys of Enoch*, which states that we are cosmic citizens, multidimensional beings, and that planet Earth was seeded with five beings of different origins.

Rather than postulate any particular theory, I would rather encourage you to keep an open mind about the entire subject. The answers to this question don't need to be known in order to keep an open mind. Just knowing that there may be other possibilities is all that is required to release judgment and fear surrounding it.

Alan believed that our souls evolved from lower beings through the millennia and was open to the other planetary influences theory. And so, I will encourage you as my mentor encouraged me to seek, experience, and find your own answers in the absence of fear or judgment.

After class, I rushed home to share the scrying technique with my family. Everyone was able to do it right away. The results stunned and shocked those who had not seen spirit before. We realized quickly that we were not only seeing past life faces but that we were also seeing spirits who took the opportunity to jump in and make themselves known.

The first time this happened, I was scrying with my husband. We were deeply entranced as we began to witness the past life faces present themselves. Suddenly, an old lady with no teeth and a concave mouth smiled at my husband and coyly turned her face. He broke his gaze because he was so alarmed and we laughed thinking that it was one of my previous lifetimes. My husband even joked about seeing that old lady's toothless smile when he thought of me.

This was the first time that we noticed a spirit face move. When I told Alan what had happened, he immediately identified that it was not one of my past life identities but rather the spirit of an old lady. He said that when a spirit face moves or tries to communicate, it is an actual spirit or ghost. The energy produced through scrying induces a higher frequency that enables spirits to become visible. The spirit world can see the light created through the technique and will often take the opportunity to step in and make contact.

That is why it is very important to protect yourself, set your intention of who you will allow to come forward, and clear your energy field after each session. Setting intention simply means to have a clear and focused idea about what the desired outcome will be. You'll find information on how to clear energy in chapter 8.

One evening, my family was sitting around the pool and we decided to do some scrying sessions. Without a thought, my husband grabbed the camera and began taking pictures of us in action. When we finished, he began to review the photographs with sheer bewilderment. We discovered that we were not only able to see the spirit faces during the session but we were also able to capture them on film!

I contacted Alan again to discuss our strange and anomalous photographs. He admitted that he had never thought to photograph a session and was eager to see what we had captured. After carefully reviewing our photographs, he concluded that we were onto something big.

As I began to fall asleep that night, a thought popped into my head that made me jump from slumber and run full throttle across the house. A synchronicity so amazing that I could not ignore it or wait for morning to explore. The image of a book hovered in my mind. One that I had purchased the previous year and had added to my collection of other bound treasures. I knew I would not sleep until I found this particular book.

My husband was still whirling from my leap out of bed when I returned with book in hand. I had found it: *Spirit Faces* written by Mark Macy. His book indicates that by standing beside a large generator and utilizing the increased energy output, spirit faces could be photographed on an individual. His book includes many spirit photographs taken in that manner. I knew that a connection had been made between his research and what we had discovered with scrying. Was it possible that a human being had the ability to increase their energy without a generator, just through concentration? Was concentration enough to drop the veil and enter the frequency of spirit? The answer was a resounding YES. We were collectively obtaining proof. Humans can achieve a very high vibration through simple meditation and concentration.

All of us are like walking generators. The human energy field is largely misunderstood and is mostly used at minimal capacity. We all have unlimited ability to harness energy for many things, including healing and spirit communication.

Unfortunately, Alan passed away shortly after my training with him. For the next decade, I continued to work with the scrying technique that Alan had taught me and shared it with students and friends all over the world. Oftentimes, the spirit of my mentor would appear during class to show his approval and gratitude.

The scrying technique had taught my eyes to see spiritually, and I began to see spirit faces more regularly during normal daily activities. This ability allowed me to become more aware of the spirit world and see when a person had a loved one in spirit with them.

If you develop your skills for scrying, it is possible that you may gain the ability to see your loved ones in spirit too. I have seen people shift into another person midway through conversation and recognized this experience as a past life revealing itself. The effect was only temporary but allowed me to understand more about a person by taking in all other lifetimes that had contributed to their patterns and choices. I was able to become more compassionate toward others because of this new perspective. The more I learned about the phenomenon, the more it taught me to expand my spiritual sight and awareness of spirit.

Scrying has enhanced my work as a medium, as a healer, and as a human being. Scrying may reveal things to you that you have never seen before and this can expand your own understanding of the world and your place in it. Scrying to see spirit is an ancient art, but it is your divine right to use and to develop it as a gift.

As you read this book and practice the techniques, it is advised that you master scrying first before you embark on transfiguration. Transfiguration is a term most often used by the Spiritualists to convey the ability to see spirits on the face of an advanced medium. This may occur in a séance setting but may also be demonstrated to a group of sitters. As you advance to transfiguration, more expertise is required to hold energy solo and for longer periods of time. By practicing the mediumship scrying technique first, you will learn to hold your energy at a higher frequency, thus preparing yourself to see spirit. Work with scrying until you are able to get consistent results before moving on to transfiguration.

Physical Mediumship

The most common form of mediumship is mental mediumship, which occurs in the mind of the medium. This is usually associated with channeling, where a spirit will impress their personality and deliver a message through the thoughts of the medium.

Physical mediumship produces physical results, which simply means that something takes place that can be seen, heard, or felt. It can also include the movement of a physical item. Both the mediumship scrying and transfigure techniques are considered forms of physical mediumship.

Mediumship works differently with every person. Everyone has some mediumship ability, some stronger than others.

Oftentimes, mediumship abilities are shut down or discouraged, but it is not too late to go back and develop those innate abilities that may have been blocked for years. Some mediums may have the ability to see spirits with their physical eyes, while most will see, hear, and feel spirits intuitively. The spirit world often conveys messages through symbols, and those may vary from medium to medium.

Would it surprise you to learn that most mediums have not actually seen a spirit? Or that the many paranormal investigators who seek spirit contact (no matter how devoted) may have never seen a ghost? What if these simple little secrets, learning how to mediumship scry and transfigure, could change that for you? In the following chapters I will discuss how to do this, but in this chapter I will get to the core of why people want to see spirit and then talk about what may be blocking you from doing so.

You may encounter people who have reservations, disbelief, or fear surrounding the spirit world, but don't let that discourage you. I have found that even trained mediums will allow themselves to experience spirits intuitively but may still carry fear about *seeing* spirits with their physical eyes. I would like to explore that fear in an effort to release it before you attempt to make spirit contact.

There are many spiritual planes and the spirit world has a vast assortment of energetic beings that exist at different frequencies. When you begin to peer through the veil, you may see many of these different beings. It is important to note that they exist with us and around us whether we can see them or not. Some beings will be our own loved ones;

you may see angels and spirit guides and you may see other entities entirely.

It is the other entities that provoke the most fear in people and may prevent them from embarking on developing their spiritual sight. Personally, I would rather see what energies are around me and my loved ones rather than remain in the dark. With knowledge, comes power. You may always clear the energy field of yourself or someone else to send away entities that are not beneficial (see chapter 8).

Today's mediums vary widely in their approach to spirit communication. In the United States, mediumship has grown in popularity, mostly due to famous celebrity mediums featured on television shows. It is nearly impossible to enter a metaphysical store without glancing upon a dozen or more business cards with people claiming to be mediums. It seems that everyone wants to be a medium these days and the discerning factor in choosing one comes down to experience. Some people who market themselves as mediums may still be early in their development and may not have the ability to connect with spirit as well as a more seasoned and dedicated medium devoted to the work. While mediumship is a divine gift that is inherent in all people, it must be developed and nurtured to reach its full potential.

Even when people spontaneously open up to the spirit world and begin to see spirits, there is much to learn about the spirit world before they are equipped to work with the public. This ability is often considered a gift that keeps giving throughout your lifetime. The more time you spend developing your ability, the more you will be rewarded with clear and accurate messages.

Being called a medium typically means that you have chosen to use your gifts of connecting to the spirit world to help others connect with loved ones who have passed. Some mediums enjoy a spirit-filled life without extending their gifts to help others communicate. They may feel the frequency of spirit around them and take cues to help them discern what job to take or how to handle an issue in their lives. It is not required that every medium works with the public. The choice is a personal one. What you decide to do with your gift is entirely up to you and there is no wrong choice.

In the United Kingdom, mediums are formerly schooled and spend many years in devoted service to their development as a medium. They mainly work on platform (or what we call gallery style in the United States): This is where a medium will stand on stage in front of a small or large gathering and deliver messages from spirit to the crowd. The demonstrations are public, low-priced, and are offered at a weekly service in church. Some mediums also work with private clients in one-on-one sessions. They are usually registered in the *Spiritualist National Union,* which was developed to oversee the work of practicing mediums operating within the spiritualist community. There are several spiritualist camps operating in the United States: the two most known are in Lilydale, New York, and Cassadaga, Florida. The Arthur Findlay College is an entire campus designated for the Development of Psychic Sciences and the Advancement of Spiritualism and is located in Stansted, England.

Many people refer to a "natural medium" as a person who was born with the ability to see spirit. Oftentimes, this ability is inherited from an ancestor who did the development and forged a new receptiveness into the family gene pool. Natural mediums often claim to see, hear, and feel spirits from an early age without any formal training.

As the natural medium grows up, this ability can be deteriorated by their family or community if they are in fear about it, thinking that it is against their religion. This type of fear has been bred by dominating religions that did not want people to gain their own connection, but rather rely solely upon the church for guidance. The whole idea of people being able to connect with spirit, angels, and guides for themselves caused some religious leaders to fear losing followers and a possibility that the church would cease to exist.

Throughout human history, people have demonstrated a very natural ability to connect with the spirit world and communicate with the hierarchy of spirit, angels, and guides. In every culture, race, and part of the world, these people have existed, and for the most part, have been regarded by their community with respect. In some cultures, they were known as the seers, elders, wise men and wise women, medicine men/women, oracles, visionaries, prophets, healers, and, of course, witches.

Many people have an inherent fear about using their abilities due to the long and nefarious history of persecution of those with psychic powers and mediumistic abilities. In some parts of the world, this is still occurring. These tragedies impart a deep fear that may also be inherited from ancestors and absorbed through group consciousness. For instance, if you had an ancestor who was punished or ostracized for demonstrating mediumistic abilities, you may have inherited the receptivity to spirit along with fear surrounding your ability to use it. This fear is one of the things that may stand in the way of a person looking to explore their own gift of mediumship or seek the guidance from one.

As technology advances, the ability to connect with the spirit world is quickly gaining validation. Some ancient cultures feared what they did not understand and considered mediumship as some sort of devilish energy that must be evil simply because it lacked explanation. Thankfully, those belief systems are being eliminated through advances in science and a better understanding of the mind and human energy field. A variety of paranormal devices have helped to document spirit activity, including capturing voice recordings, apparitions, and the movement of physical objects. The electroencephalogram (EEG) has been used to measure and record electrical activity in the brain. This can indicate brain wave patterns and changes in brain activity while doing meditation and tapping into higher levels of consciousness. The quantitative electroencephalogram (qEEG) analyzes electrical activity of the brain during what is known as a brain scan.

In 2013, the television show *Dr. Oz* revealed a scientific experiment using the quantitative electroencephalogram on the *Long Island Medium* Theresa Caputo. The results indicated that when Theresa was connected to spirit and channeling a message (mental mediumship) the right hemisphere of her brain was activated. Dr. Amen, who administered the test, also mentioned research from Canada that is being used to expand perception by stimulating the right temporal lobe. The results were that people reported feelings of a presence, which they believed to be God or spirit, during the experiment. This type of research suggests that something very real is happening to the performing medium. A physical change occurs that can be seen and measured on the brain scan.

It is a testament to the human spirit that mediumship survived long before science was willing to validate it and through all the religious domination and persecution. I would like to give thanks to the many mediums who continued to be of service to the spirit world at tremendous personal cost to themselves and family. Their resilience and dedication have ushered in a more open-minded reality for us all.

Perhaps now is the time for us to heal the universal scars acquired through history and really embrace the spirit world with love instead of fear. Believing that life exists after death can greatly impact the way you live your daily life by feeling greater peace and a larger sense of purpose in connection to the cycle of life. The spirit world is real and our loved ones never leave us. We, each and every one of us, can learn to tap into higher frequencies without fear and we can learn to see spirits. We can become mediums to help others communicate with loved ones. We can become that bridge of light to help foster healing for those left in grief.

Nearly every religion and culture from around the globe acknowledges that the spirit world exists, and many cultures actually employ spirit communication in every aspect of their daily lives. In some parts of China, where Buddhism is more prevalent, the spirits of ancestors are treated like living members of the family. They treat spirits with respect and honor while still setting out places for them to sit at the family dinner table. They consult with their ancestors for help in every area of their lives. There are some Japanese customs of pleasing the spirits of the deceased through making offerings. The Native Americans consulted with Shaman or Medicine Men for communication with their ancestor spirits, who offered advice about weather, where to hunt, and even battle.

Shintoism, a Japanese religion, believes in spirits that linger after the body dies. The Polynesian cultures of the South Pacific often pay respect to their ancestor spirits, believing also that mana or spirit energy is infused in all things. Aborigine people also believe that ancestor spirits exist and that everything has spirit energy, including all trees, rocks, and things. Hinduism, Buddhism, and Judaism all teach that ghosts exist.

When you see, hear, or feel the spirit of a deceased loved one, there is no denying it. Every spirit has a unique energy signature that is the same as when the person was living. This energy cannot be duplicated and when you encounter it, you will know the experience to be authentic because you will recognize it and feel it in your heart.

The techniques offered in this book, scrying and transfiguration, will enable you to see spiritually and will help you to connect with the spirit world in a dramatically new way. Before you learn to do so, it is important to release any fear and trauma you have about mediumship and connecting with spirit.

Meditation to Release Trauma

Lay down comfortably on your back with a small pillow under your knees. Close your eyes and relax. You may hold quartz crystals or any crystal that you feel drawn to. If you like incense and candlelight, this will help create a meditative environment. You may also play very quiet music or nature sounds in the background while you travel. Now, go ahead and take a deep breath in and then blow it out through pursed lips. Repeat two more times. Feel your body relax.

Imagine going deep within Mother Earth and anchoring your energy there. Bring the energy from Mother Earth up through the bottom of your feet and up through each of the main chakras, opening and balancing each one as the energy rises. The main chakras are at the base of the spine (root chakra), just below the belly button (sacral chakra), just above the belly button (solar plexus chakra), the center of your chest (heart chakra), the throat chakra, the forehead area (third eye), and then finally at the top of your head (crown chakra). Bring the energy out through the crown chakra and far above your space to connect with the heavens. You will feel a deep sense of relaxation and connectedness as you are connected from below and above with energy moving through your whole being.

While you are connected to the energy of Creator/God/Universe ask to be granted access to each and every situation that created trauma for you regarding the spirit world. You may be shown images of yourself as a child, hiding under the covers because you saw things that could not be explained by the grown-ups. You may see a different version of you experiencing pain due to your abilities. Allow yourself to witness these events in rapid succession without feeling any of the emotions; just watch the movie play quickly in your mind, alerting you to times and places that your soul stored this trauma. Now, with a very firm conviction, say to yourself:

"It is now time to gently release these traumas. I thank myself for creating blocks to protect me from my spiritual gifts, but I am now capable of accessing all of my divine gifts with safety. Please release all trauma stored deep within my DNA and all painful memories associated with these events from past, present, and future lives as well as any place in time/space that I exist. Allow healing to come in and take the place of these memories, providing me with comfort, safety, stability, and a true connection to divine energy. I trust Creator/God/Universe to make these changes in my highest and best way and reclaim any senses/gifts/abilities that were given in exchange. I release the need to hold these traumas in all past, present, and future lives. It is my divine right to be fully connected without fear. Anchor in any lessons that I learned through experiencing these traumas and release all hurt, sorrow, and resentments toward people who may have interacted with me in a harmful manner due to my abilities. I send them forgiveness for not knowing better. As my gifts are restored, the power inside me increases with integrity, light, and compassion. I observe my energy being restored as all my intuitive gifts are activated in my highest and best way now."

Lie still and allow this process to complete within you. Give thanks when you are done.

Why Do People Want to See Spirits?

Why do people want to see spirits? What drives them to want to connect with the spirit world and make contact with their loved ones? The reasons are many and vary from individual to individual. The fact is: Life on earth is limited. Eventually, we will all pass away and leave this physical world. Our loved ones will perish and we will be affected by death in countless ways. This is not a bad thing; it is simply a fact of living.

Fear of Death

Sometimes people have such a fear of death that they do not fully appreciate the gift of life. People can spend their entire life being so afraid of death that they do not take chances, risk falling in love, travel to places they dream of, or fully reach their potential. This fear can halt people in their tracks as they cling to the familiar, the safe, and the known. It can cause a person to live a life full of routine and pattern where their soul ceases to flourish in the daily miracle of living. Perhaps these people also fear the unknown and wonder what comes next, which often accompanies the fear of death. When these people have the opportunity to see and experience spirit, they are profoundly changed with the knowledge that something else exists. Knowing that their life matters and what they do affects the world, their loved ones, and their spirit brings tremendous peace.

We came to this life to do something and I can guarantee you it was not to hold down a 9-5 job and simply go through the motions of life set up by daily routine. We came here to learn, grow, love, and experience all that life has to offer. We came here to challenge ourselves, appreciate the beauty, make changes, inspire others, and create. When people who have a fear of death learn to see spirits, they often have a much deeper appreciation of life. The experience often marks the beginning of their life being fully lived, and for this, it is truly beneficial. When a person knows there is something that occurs after this physical life, they accept that they are spiritual beings inhabiting a physical body, and because of this can do extraordinary things.

Curiosity

Some people aren't driven by the need to know what happens after death. They are just simply curious, doubtful, or skeptical, and wish to experience spirit communication for themselves. That is perfectly fine. It is a fundamental part of being human that we ask questions and want to experience things for ourselves.

Being able to experience the spirit world can enrich your life in many ways. It can be fun and exciting and may open doors of possibilities for you. You may gain insight into your own belief system and find a renewed sense of purpose. There is nothing in life that does not serve you because you learn from everything you do, see, hear, and experience. If you are just curious, you, too, can benefit from connecting with the spirit world.

Loss of a Loved One

The most common reason for people desiring to connect with the spirit world is the loss of a loved one. For some, this desire did not exist before the loss occurred. It is very typical for grief to be the catalyst for growth and spiritual expansion.

When a person dies, they leave behind many loved ones who are all affected by the passing in different ways. Some people become overcome by grief and have a difficult time finding the desire to live without their loved one. For others, there is an ache in their heart that never goes away. It seems that the closer the relationship, the more difficult it is to heal from. Survivors are often left with feelings of being abandoned, or left to live their life without their partner. They may feel angry, or even blame God for their loss. These are all normal phases of grief and it is important to release any guilt you may have in association with these feelings.

Many people feel haunted by not having the opportunity to say goodbye to their loved ones when they pass. If you fall into this category, let me share something that I have come to learn through working with thousands of spirits over a lifetime. Our loved ones choose many aspects of their departure, including who is with them when they pass. It is common for people to be gathered at the deathbed waiting for their loved one to take their last breath when suddenly they are called away for a moment. When they return, they find that their loved one passed when they were away. Please do not feel tormented by this as it was by design. Sometimes your loved ones don't want you to see them die. They don't want you to experience this event and sometimes find it easier to go without worrying about how it will affect you. If your loved one chose to leave without you being present, know that everything about their passing was meant to be. You weren't supposed to be there, otherwise you would have been. It is not a punishment, you did not let them down and there is nothing you could have done differently. Every soul has experiences that they came here to fulfill, and that includes many aspects of their passing.

When a passing seems too early or particularly tragic, there is a reason for it. I have been shown extreme cases where violence has taken the life of children and their soul knew the event was going to happen in advance. I have also been shown that special transition angels show up to help them through the process by telling them when it is time for their spirit to leave their body moments before the injury, gunshot, or accident occurs. They literally feel no pain and do not suffer.

For parents or close family members, the final moments of such a death seem to prevent them from healing because of how tragic the experience was. Every situation is unique with a variety of lessons that may be gleaned once the deep grief and blame are released. With violence, people will blame the perpetrator but also blame themselves for not protecting their loved one better. The self-blame must be released in order to heal.

It is difficult to think of children as being wise souls, but this is how they present themselves when I connect to their spirit. We often forget that in the cycle of death and rebirth, our soul is infinite and we think of our young as playful children visiting earth for the first time. When in reality, their little body houses an infinitely wise soul; sometimes, with a big mission to bring change or awareness for the rest of society. Many families are moved to help create new laws and discover a new life purpose in helping a cause after being affected by such an event. It can be particularly difficult to make sense out of a tragic and senseless act that causes so much suffering.

I have found that the people who recover and learn to embrace their life again are those who seek healing and purpose. Oftentimes, this reclamation of life comes with a new zest that is inspired by the loss. It's as if the survivors know their loved one is whole and at peace and wants them to release the tragedy so that they can live again.

I am in no way suggesting that this is easy, but it is possible. When you establish contact with your loved one in spirit, this can be especially healing—to see that the loved ones are okay and are by your side, loving you, comforting you, and wanting you to find the strength to love and laugh. Every time you choose joy, their spirit feels better and it becomes easier for them to reconnect with you.

Many people long to say they're sorry once someone in their life passes. They beat themselves up and harbor regret for not being able to apologize to someone until it is too late. I know from experience that it is never too late. I have seen spirits heal and go into the light when their living loved ones forgive them. I have also seen people heal tremendously when they apologize to the spirit of a loved one after they pass. The healing can work both ways. When you speak, your loved ones in spirit hear you. They know what you hold in your heart and probably already forgave you. The process of reconnecting can help validate that the forgiveness has been accepted. It is never too late to make things right. While the spirit world is quick to forgive and release painful memories, the living may find it more difficult. Making amends may be part of this healing for you. See if there is something you can do to bring healing to the situation. Meditate or pray for an answer that will bring healing for all parties.

One of the most common things that people regret not saying enough is "I love you." For some reason, many people live and die with all this love being left on the table. In other words, they fear sharing their true feeling with another person when they are living and then find that it is too late to express their feelings when the loved one dies. If life teaches us anything, it is that life is short. Our physical experiences are designed to be rather short so that our soul can grow. Our lessons are often found in missed opportunities, particularly when it comes to expressing our love. In addition to that, our missed opportunities are often the reasons why our descendants do better at certain things than we did. When we connect with spirit, we have that opportunity to express the love we withheld in life. And when spirit communicates, it mostly conveys the love felt for the living. You don't have to wait for spirit to show up; you can simply say that you love them at any time. The spirit world is all around you and they already know how you feel. However, being able to see spirit and convey that message can be extremely healing for both parties.

There are five well-known phases to grief that accompany the death of a loved one. The first is denial, which often sets in to help the bereaved function. During this phase, there is emptiness, numbness, and not knowing how to make sense of things. There may be feelings of not wanting to go on living after the loss and not knowing how to.

The second phase of grief is anger. The survivor may lash out at family and friends or become consumed in looking for someone to blame for the loss. The anger can be turned inward on themselves or may be directed at God for allow-ing this death to occur. Sometimes, family and friends don't know what to do when they encounter this anger and feel beat up emotionally by the very person they are trying to support. This is a phase, so please be gentle with the bereaved and do NOT take their anger personally at this point. It is very important that the anger be allowed to be felt so that it is not stuffed down where it can deteriorate the health and well-being of the person grieving.

Bargaining is the third phase of grief. Often people will try to bargain with God to bring back their loved one if they make changes in their life. It is important to recognize that these feelings may be present in those moving through grief and to understand how raw and vulnerable they can be feeling.

The fourth phase is depression and this is often felt when the bereaved realizes that none of their bargaining worked. They are left with the unmovable notion that they will never see their loved one again and that they are left alone to pick up the pieces of their life. They don't know how to do this, or if they can. This feeling can be so overwhelming that they often don't know if they want to get through it and live life without their loved one. Again, this phase is absolutely nor-mal and should be accepted rather than feared. Know that it is a phase and with the proper love and support, it will lessen over time.

Even if there are no loved ones nearby who understand what you are going through, the love and support can be found within. You can love and support yourself through this by un-derstanding how normal it is and that there is nothing wrong with you. Oftentimes, friends and family lack the patience and awareness about how grief works and they want to see you feel better again. They may push you to be happy before you are capable of feeling that way. Know that your loved ones are only doing what they think will help you because they are worried that they are in danger of losing you.

Depression may show up as a lack of enthusiasm for life, not wanting to leave the house, not wanting to get out of bed, or the inability to stop crying. This is normal and the more you allow yourself to feel this, the quicker this phase of grief will be released. If there is an extended duration of this phase, I would recommend joining a grief support group or seeing a specialist that deals with grief and soul healing.

The next and final phase of grief is acceptance. During this phase, plans for moving forward can be made. The grief does not fully go away but it lessens over time. During the acceptance phase, there is an understanding about the loss, but there is also the strength to go on. During all the phases, it is normal to ask for your loved one in spirit to reconnect with you. When the grief is the heaviest, it will most likely not happen because your own energy is blocking it. As you move into acceptance, your energy is relieved of the heaviness of anger and depression and begins to heal and feel more positive about living.

The accepted and traditional view of dealing with grief ends with the last phase of acceptance. However, I have found that there is one more. This is typically when a person will begin to experience their loved one in spirit. Oftentimes, this will happen spontaneously when you are alone. It is common for the spirit of a loved one to visit you while you sleep. You may wake up and see an apparition in your doorway or feel their loving touch on your cheek. You may hear their voice or begin to receive signs from them when they are around you.

I will call this the spirit visit phase. I really feel that this is the phase that completes the grieving process and is the one that stays with you for the duration of your life. This phase is magical and meaningful because you become aware that your loved one is still with you. When you think about your loved one, you often get a sign right away that makes you smile or feel reconnected. You may see an image or hear a song that reminds you of them at exactly the same time that you were thinking of them. You know that they still exist and that they look after you. You can often feel them around you and know that they want you to be happy again. They love you so much that they will be present with you as you ride through this grief process and make it out okay. In fact, they will stay with you in spirit forever.

As your grief begins to heal, your loved one in spirit is released to do what they need to do on the other side. However, they are just a thought away. When you miss them or call out to them, they hear you and can reconnect instantly. They enjoy being with you but don't want to hold you back from the necessary elements of moving on either. Their visits will be less and less noticeable but that is simply because they don't want to prevent you from having new experiences and expanding into new relationships. They are still with you but at a frequency that is not as easily felt by the living. They will always be with you to see that you embrace living again and that you thrive.

For many people, this is the time when they seek out mediums or venture into spirit communication. They have usually had some of their own experiences with the spirit world and seek to understand more.

Don't worry about asking to connect with loved ones too often. Like I said, they are with you all the time. They will continue to share your life experiences with you and may even choose to be one of your spirit guides. If this is the case, their spirit will be very present in your life and you will feel that connection every day of your life.

When I decided to work as a medium, I had two loved ones in spirit who were my catalysts. My little sister Mary and my best friend Dickie both passed away within two years of each other, and both committed to helping me understand the spirit world so that I could help teach and heal other people as a medium. They show up every time I work with people and they encourage me to live my life to the fullest. Mary imparts her gentleness and love for nature and animals while Dickie's influence is all about laughter and seeking new friendships and exploration. Their lives were very different but they offer their expertise to help enhance my life in unexpected ways.

As you move into the spirit visit phase, you will seek fun ways to reconnect with your loved ones and benefit from knowing that they are with you. In this way, you will become a catalyst for other people to heal and live life to the fullest as they seek to experience the joy of reconnection.

In the next chapter, you will learn how to connect to spirit, no matter the reason, through scrying.

Scrying

The term scrying comes from the English word "descry," meaning to make out dimly or to reveal. Scrying is a form of divination often used to predict future events or assist with clairvoyant abilities. It is associated with crystal balls, black onyx mirrors, clouds, or reading tea leaves. Scrying may be used to see into the past or to give clarity to a current life situation. Many cultures around the world have practiced different forms of scrying. It was once believed that scrying was the product of either gods or the devil, and some cultures feared using the technique. Modern-day beliefs support the awareness of other dimensions in time and space and have greatly released any superstitions regarding use of this ancient technique. It is now believed that scrying in any form creates a stillness of mind and allows you to access and interpret subtle energy, and experience increased awareness of spirit as you release any occupation with the physical dimension.

Learning to scry can be fun, but it can also help develop your interpretive abilities and your spiritual sight. The spirit world often conveys messages through symbolism and the very nature of it seeks interpretation. The better you are at different types of scrying, the easier it will be to understand the messages that spirit sends you. We live in an interactive world filled with hidden messages that can help alert us to danger or guide us toward success. These abilities are your divine right to reclaim and use in your daily life. The following methods can help accelerate your progress in working with the spirit world.

Clearing your space prior to a session is as important as clearing it when you finish. Prior to your spiritual work, the process is simpler and will ensure that you are connecting to your intended in spirit and not any leftover residual energy. It is always advised to set your intention (see chapter 1) and say a prayer of some kind. You may say whatever feels powerful and right for you based on your personal belief system. In my suggested prayers, I use the word Creator to encompass the energy of all creation and not one particular god associated with religion. Here is a prayer for clearing space:

"Creator, it is commanded to clear this space of any residual energy and low vibrational frequencies that are not in my highest and best. Fill this space with unconditional love and light, allowing spirit to communicate with grace and ease. Thank you."

As you become better at connecting and disconnecting with the spirit world, you will be able to do it with your intention and your mind. However, as you move through the ranks of beginner to intermediate, it is best to follow all of the guidance and apply tools to assist you.

Clearing Space

The purpose of clearing space is to prepare the room for spiritual work. It is important to create a sacred space or "clear space" so that any spiritual work you do is not contaminated by existing energy. Have you ever entered a room shortly after an argument and felt the angry energy lingering in the air? Or have you entered a cathedral, church, or prayer circle in nature and experienced an almost instant "holy" feeling or a peaceful state of mind? The energy around us is constantly being charged by our emotions and events that occur. That energy becomes like a blueprint and can define a place over time.

Spirits exist around us at all times as well. They tend to match our frequency and may go unnoticed. However, sometimes, we can attract some not-so-nice spirits or unhealed ones that simply need our help to move on. These spiritual energies can also get entangled in our energy field and the space we occupy. For clarity and discernment, it serves to clear the space of all residual emotions and spiritual energies to begin with a clean slate. Below are some suggested tools to aid in the process.

Sage

Burn sage prior to your sitting. This helps to purify the energy of the room and protect it. Burning sage can disallow or drive out negative spirits. It will still allow spirits of ancestors to come through with messages of love.

Sweet Grass

Sweet grass is often used after sage and/or cedar. Once a space has been cleared and purified, the burning of sweet grass invites in good spirits. This would include your spirit guide team that assists with your spiritual development as well as loved ones in spirit.

Cedar

Burning cedar cleanses the energy in the room, and it clears negative energy and spirits as it purifies the space to be used for sacred purposes. Helps to purify and clear the air and may be desired in cases where people are sensitive to sage burning. (You may use this before and/or after a sitting.)

Frankincense

Frankincense is a very powerful incense and is used to raise the vibration in the room, creating a sacred space. You can also apply Frankincense essential oil to the medium or sitters to protect spiritually and aid with spiritual connection.

Tibetan Tingsha Bells

Tingsha bells are made from two metal cymbals connected by a leather strap. When you clang them together, the chime created is a high-pitched tone that is valuable for clearing space. These are wonderful to use before and after a sitting.

Holy Water or Blessed Water

Holy water can be used to help elevate and protect a space. It can also be applied directly to the medium or sitters as well as sprayed into the room or rubbed onto the walls.

Prayer

Prayer or meditation are recommended as well and can be as simple as asking for your highest and best, working with light beings, ascended masters, and loved ones in spirit. Depending on your spiritual preference, you may ask for whomever you wish to oversee the process, ensuring positive and healing results. Many people call upon their own spirit team, which may include ancestor spirits as well as Archangels, Mother Mary, Jesus, Buddha, Vishnu, Shiva, or the Creator God. Reciting well-known prayers can help clear and elevate a space as well.

Now that you and your space are cleared and ready to begin, you will learn how to scry.

Techniques and Tools for Scrying

Pendulum

One of the easiest tools to use for developing your scrying abilities is the pendulum. Though the pendulum will not directly affect your ability to see spiritually, it will help you to interpret the subtle energy around you. The pendulum is used for divination and healing as well.

A pendulum is most often a natural stone or crystal; however, it can be made from any material. They are usually the shape of an ice cream cone with a pointed tip at the bottom. The chain or string is approximately six inches long with a ball or knot at the end to hold on to.

When you select your pendulum, it is important to do so in person rather than online. Allow yourself to be intuitively drawn to the one that stands out to you. When you hold the ball or knot, allow the pendulum to tangle over the open-faced palm of your opposite hand. If you are right handed, hold on to the pendulum with the tip of your right thumb and index finger. If you are left handed, use your left index finger and thumb. Tell the pendulum to show you "yes" and then wait for a response. This is a simple test that is similar to taking a car on a test drive.

Just because the pendulum you selected may be your favorite stone, it may not necessarily work well with you. I have selected pendulums based on the beauty of the stone and felt disappointed when they were totally unresponsive to me. When you ask the pendulum to show you "yes" it should begin to move. It may move directly forward and back in the direction of a nodding head. Once you have allowed the pendulum to show you "yes," ask it to show you "no." This often will be a movement from side to side (left and then right).

There is no wrong or right way, as long as you can interpret what the movement means and that it is consistent. My pendulum moves in a clockwise circle for yes and counter clockwise for no. If the pendulum you selected is unresponsive, put it back and select another one. Continue doing this until you find a pendulum that resonates well to your frequency and moves about freely for you.

Once you have selected the right pendulum for you it will be important to charge it with your energy. This can be achieved by carrying it with you for a few days, sleeping with it under your pillow, or doing a blessing on it. I advise doing all of the above. A simple blessing may be said as you hold your pendulum in the palm of your hand.

Here is an example of a simple blessing to clear and charge your pendulum:

"Creator, I call upon you, my angels, and my highest guides to restore the energy of this pendulum, clearing any residual energy from anyone who handled it previously. Infuse this pendulum with light and love for accurate readings. Thank you."

Now, your pendulum is ready for use. Many people enjoy the efficiency of working with a pendulum because it can help produce quick yes and no answers to the questions you have. The pendulum is primarily moved through your own subconscious thoughts in a process called ideomotor. This means that the ego and conscious mind are taken out of the equation to allow your subconscious mind to affect the involuntary movement of the pendulum. The subconscious thought is translated through your fingertips, causing motion in the pendulum, even though your hand remains still.

The spirit world is made up of subtle energy that our conscious mind often blocks out. However, we are connected to everything around us at all times and the subconscious mind accepts this. Therefore, if we were to ask a question such as, "Is there a spiritual presence beside me?"—your conscious mind may disbelieve because it cannot see it yet, while the subconscious mind may indeed have already picked up on the presence. If the pendulum were to go forward and back or in a clockwise motion (or whatever motion was determined to be "yes" for you) then it is most likely confirming what your subconscious mind already knows. There is a spiritual presence beside you. If you think you know who it is, whether it is a deceased loved one, angel, or guide, you may ask by name if that is who is beside you. Again, you will receive a "yes" or "no" response.

Another approach to using the pendulum for spirit interaction is to use a dowsing board or spirit board with the pendulum. This can be a simple design that you draw on a piece of paper that includes all the letters of the alphabet along with numbers. When you use this method, you may ask questions and then hold your pendulum over the board. The pendulum will indicate which letter or number it means to represent as it moves in that direction and hovers over it. This is especially good when the typical yes and no question is not being used.

Using the pendulum for spirit interactions can be quite helpful. At first, you may rely upon the pendulum for answers, but with a little practice you will begin to feel the answers within your own body. This teaches you how to become more open and receptive to subtle energy in and around you.

Tea Leaves

Tea leaf reading is known as tasseography. It was first used by fortune-tellers in medieval Europe who interpreted splattered wax to predict future events. The practice later evolved to using tea leaves, coffee grounds, and even wine sediment. Tea leaf readings are an ancient form of scrying that enable you to access knowledge about the past, present, and future. Many cultures still use tea leaf readings in modern times.

The process is simple and entirely interpretive, so practice will enable you to gain confidence with it. You will want to use loose tea and not a tea bag. Once the hot water has steeped long enough, hold your tea cup and think about what issue you seek clarity about. Quiet your mind as you reflect on your situation and be open to what guidance you receive. Then drink your tea, leaving the leaf remnants inside the bottom of your tea cup. At this time, you may scry into the tea cup to get your answer. As you gaze upon the tea leaves, notice any familiar shapes that stand out. You may notice more than one image or the entire contents could represent something that you identify as significant. Ask yourself if there are any numbers, letters, faces, animals, or images that can bring forth the answer you seek. For instance, if you see what looks like an airplane, perhaps this indicates travel coming up for you. An unexpected trip or visitor.

Some people like to swirl their tea intermittently as they drink it while focusing on the answer they seek. When the liquid is gone and only the tea leaves remain, turn the cup upside down and dump them onto the saucer. This process may make it easier for viewing, but there is no wrong way to do it. Scry upon the leaf remnants and in the same way as previously mentioned, look for images or shapes that stand out to you. It is possible that you could even feel a message without identifying one particular image within the tea. Pay attention to any feelings you have as you sit quietly, looking upon the remnants.

You could make this process as simple or as complicated as you wish. Just remember that this should be regarded as a ritual of sorts and care should be taken to keep the process pure. Always ask to be shown what is in your highest and best interest and the good for all concerned. Keep in mind that the future can be changed as it is constantly being created and re-created by your current choices. If you see something that you wish to change, take the steps to change it now and then review a new tea leaf reading at a later date to validate that the changes have taken place.

Cloud Scrying

Cloud scrying was used by many ancient cultures and is still used today. Perhaps because it is the most accessible form of scrying that can be achieved from just about anywhere and no tools are required. The ancient Celtic Druids employed cloud scrying to increase their intuition and receive spiritual messages for insight into harvest, battle, and spiritual knowledge. Most of you have probably done this at some point in your life and may or may not have known that this was an actual form of scrying.

You may do this by gazing out the window of an airplane or lying on the grass on a warm afternoon watching the clouds move. Ask a question or set an intention for what you want answers to before you begin. Allow your mind to relax as you peer into the clouds above and watch them as they move and shift across the sky. Many images will appear and these can be considered symbols or messages from spirit. Oftentimes, people will see something entirely different from the person scrying right beside them, and that is okay. Whatever you see is meant for you, so do not look for validation from others. You may also receive impressions or have a sense of inner knowing about a situation that you were seeking answers to. Some important leaders have noted that they were seeking guidance during battle and looked to the clouds when the answers came to them, leading them to victory. This form of scrying can be deeply meditative and can help to slow down your mind to help you receive spiritual guidance.

My daughter and I have often enjoyed cloud scrying in the late afternoon while lying on the ground and gazing upon the clouds as we talk. The entire process is calming and brings about clarity even when an actual image has not been perceived from the clouds. If you watch carefully, you may see quite a few images take form as they gently move and transform into different shapes. Go within yourself as you consider what the meaning may be for you.

Recently, I looked up and saw the image of a leg and foot protruding out of a cloud. This image may mean that it is time to take another step forward on a project or certain juncture in your life. For some, it may indicate that exercise is needed and a daily walk would be beneficial. For someone else, it may relate to a recent injury of the leg or foot, indicating that spirit knows what you seek healing for. The possibilities are endless, so allow the process to expand within you and bring forward its relevance in your life. Always give thanks for any messages or guidance you receive.

Crystal Ball

For many of you, a crystal ball brings to mind images of the Wicked Witch of the West from the *Wizard of Oz*. I always remember the scene with the flying monkeys and how she can see what is happening to the sweet, unsuspecting Dorothy. Although it is entirely possible to see visual images within a crystal ball, most of the time this technique will enhance your ability to tune in with your own receptive abilities to perceive what is happening in the past, present, and future. You may be able to see images as you gaze at the crystal ball or you may tune into a sort of movie that plays in your mind's eye as the crystal ball serves as more of a focal point rather than a movie screen.

A crystal ball is often made of glass or clear quartz crystal, but may be made of any type of stone. It has been called a shew stone, which is actually an archaic word for show stone. It was called this because the sitter would scry into the stone to be "shown" the answers. Although clear crystal balls are more traditional, I have found myself drawn to a cherry quartz, which has red hues mixed with clear. It has very interesting features, which helps to captivate my interest while using it to hold my focus and quiet my mind. I have used this stone for crystal grid layouts as well so it has multiple purposes. Cherry quartz has all the qualities of quartz, making it perfect to use for healing or meditation. It clears energy blocks and helps to balance the spiritual, physical, emotional, and mental planes. Quartz is used to aid with clarity and amplify energy. The cherry quartz has additional properties that are beneficial for the heart chakra and bringing emotional balance and love.

In selecting your own crystal ball, I would recommend that you shop in person so that you can hold it in your hands and connect to the energy of it. Typically when purchasing crystals, you should go to the one that attracts you to it. Hold it in your receptive hand (if you are right handed, hold it in your left hand and vice versa) then close your eyes. Pay attention to how your body feels when you are holding it. Crystals all have a unique frequency that affect the human energy field. Some will feel beneficial, making you feel focused and clear minded while others will make you feel drowsy or slowed down.

Crystals can help you connect to higher planes through your crown chakra or they can be very grounding, sending your energy deep within Mother Earth through your root chakra. Both qualities are important. Oftentimes, people focus so much on trying to get out of their physical body to gain a high connection that they can become airheaded or flighty. Grounding stones will help to anchor energy to create more balance while still allowing the ascent to higher consciousness. For the purposes of scrying, you may also select a crystal ball based on its overall attractiveness and interesting features. After all, you will be gazing upon it repetitively, so why not look at something that you enjoy. If it has interesting features, it will make for an excellent focal point.

Begin this process with a protection prayer of your choosing; affirming that only the highest and best comes through for all concerned. As you begin, think of what it is you would like an answer to. You may ask for communication from the spirit world or an answer about your work, relationship, or life in general. Quiet your mind as you begin to scry deeply into the crystal ball. When you begin to notice a cloudy substance form, you may either look for shapes that could be interpreted as messages or close your eyes to be shown an inner vision. It is not necessary for you to see the cloudy substance, as everyone will experience things differently. Pay attention to anything you perceive to be answers or messages while you are scrying. At times, you may feel as though you are making things up. Trust that if you have set your intention and said your protection prayers that anything you received was a gift from spirit.

When you feel you have received the answer or guidance that you were seeking, you may offer gratitude to spirit and then clear your energy. Most people like to cover their crystal ball with a sacred cloth to keep the energy pure between uses. A sacred cloth should be made of natural fibers such as cotton or silk and may be as simple or as decorative as you prefer.

Scrying Mirror

Mirror scrying actually evolved from the water scrying once used by ancient Greeks. Any mirror can be used for scrying, although some will work better than others. If you have an antique mirror with some patina, you may find more success than with a new store-bought mirror.

When we moved into our Victorian house, there was an old vanity mirror hanging over the sink in the guest bathroom. The mirror was round and hung there frameless covered with patina. My husband took it down to replace it with a more elegant framed mirror that he found at an antique store. As soon as I saw what he had done, I retrieved the old mirror and re-hung the old one in its place. There was nothing wrong with the new mirror so I didn't know why I refused the update. Thankfully, my husband has gotten used to some eccentricities in our life and sometimes having to do things that didn't make sense to him. Eventually we agreed to hang the new mirror somewhere else. I didn't know why I needed to keep that old mirror hanging in that bathroom, but it soon became evident.

Many of our guests began having strange experiences in that bathroom. While washing their hands, they would glance into the mirror and unintentionally see a spirit face looking back at them. This can be quite startling, especially when it is not expected. My daughter was washing her hands and looked up at the mirror just in time to see the entire room begin to spin. The guest bathroom had vintage wallpaper so when the pattern began to spin it was very apparent. She came out and got me right away. She didn't tell me what had happened but told me to go wash my hands and look in the mirror. I did as she asked and within a minute, the reflection of the wall behind me began to spin. I also saw the spirit of my grandma looking at me through the mirror, superimposed over my face.

Once a scrying mirror is activated, it becomes a sort of portal, and with continued use, the spirit world will become easier to connect with. If you have one of these mirrors in your house, make sure you place proper protection around it so that the portal doesn't allow anything negative to enter. This can be achieved by burning sage around the mirror and sealing it with a blessing or intention. Here is one you can use, although you may use whatever blessing or intention feels right to you:

"Creator, I ask that you clear the energy of this mirror from anything that is not in my highest and best interest. Post angels and guides to protect this portal and any energies that come through it or are reflected upon it. Allow this mirror to resonate with the highest vibration of love in the Universe. Thank you."

You may also purchase a scrying mirror at a metaphysical shop or online. There are many gifted artisans making and selling scrying mirrors on ETSY. There seems to be more of an awareness and market for scrying mirrors than in the recent past so you should be able to find one that suits you. Typically, a scrying mirror will be circular and measure six to eight inches, made from black glass or black obsidian. The shape is more of a personal preference than anything, so if you are drawn to using one that is rectangular, that is perfectly okay. A clear mirror used for scrying is more often referred to as a magic mirror, while the black shiny surface is more widely accepted as a scrying mirror.

It is possible to make your own scrying mirror by spraying the glass of a picture frame with shiny black spray paint. It usually requires four coats to be completely opaque and usable for scrying.

Say your protection prayer and then set your intention as you gaze into the mirror. Be clear whether you would like an answer to something or if you desire to connect with spirit. While you will most often see shapes or images, don't be surprised if you see spirit reflected back to you. Also, pay attention to any sensations or new thoughts that you have during this process. Spirit has a way of infusing their message into the frequency of your thoughts. The session is complete when you feel you have received your answer or connection to spirit. It may happen immediately or take some time. The scrying mirror helps to train you for seeing spirit with your physical eyes as you focus upon the reflection. When you are done, thank spirit for any cooperation and do an energy clearing on the mirror.

Water Scrying

Nostradamus used a bowl of clear water for scrying to proph-
esize future events. Some people recommend using only a
glass, brass, or silver bowl for water scrying, but I have found
that black or very dark colors work well. Fresh water from a
live stream or active body of water will often produce better results; however, with a blessing, tap water may be used.
Some people even like to add sea salt to the water as a natural
means of protection. This water may also be charged ahead
of time by allowing it to sit under the light of a full moon.

Here is a water blessing I have used, but you may say
whatever blessing resonates with you:

"Creator, cleanse this vessel and the water it contains, releasing any toxins and remnants from others. Raise the vibration to purity and perfection and allow this water to serve as
a conductor of spirit energy in my highest and best way now.
Thank you."

Set your intention of who you would like to see or what
you would like a message for. Set the bowl of water on a
steady, flat surface and begin to stare into the water. You may
look at the reflection on the surface of the water or look deep
into the bowl. Either way works fine. Still water provides a
clear, reflective surface similar to the magic mirror or mirror
scrying. The water may reveal actual faces reflected back at
you or images for you to interpret. Notice any images that
you see in the water as well as what images you perceive intuitively while you are doing this exercise, as all may be considered spirit messages.

Another approach is to set your intention and then stir
the water with a wooden spoon. This time, you will gaze into

the moving water, which is creating bubbles, ripples, and swirls. You will need a quick eye to spot the images because the view is ever changing. I prefer to use a digital camera during this process to capture the rapid images.

It helps to create an atmosphere of sacredness by burning incense and lighting candles. Be clear about what your intention is. Do you want the answer to something or do you seek proof of the afterlife and want to know if a loved one is with you? When you are ready, stir the water briskly, being careful not to splash over. You may begin taking pictures at any time and take as many as you want. Aim the camera directly at the water as it is actively whirling about. You may have to stir multiple times because the water will settle down rather quickly. Each time you stir, set or reaffirm your intention. Many symbols and even faces will appear in the photographs for you to analyze.

I have found that when a message is coming through, the whirling water will show me a variety of images. I've seen old-fashioned bicycles, cars, planes, people, and even angels. When there is no message coming through, the water looks like a blank canvas. There is a clear and discernable difference. I think you'll find that it is just as fun to interpret the photos afterward as it is to stir and gaze.

Once this water has been used, it holds a higher energy, which could be beneficial to use elsewhere. When you are finished, consider using the water for your garden or household plants rather than dumping it down the sink. Especially if you felt a connection to a loved one in spirit while using the water. Water that has been used to connect with spirit is infused with their energy and will hold that vibration. Remember, water is also a conductor of energy, so it is easier for spirits to communicate with water present. Make sure you show gratitude and then find a good use for the water.

Flame Scrying

Pyromancy or flame scrying can be done with a single candle or a large fire such as a campfire. Watching a fire burn is deeply meditative and this alone can be used to still your mind and allow guidance from spirit. Spirit often uses the flame to communicate and may blow the flame from side to side, dramatically increase the size of the flame, or completely blow the flame out. If your flame gets blown out, consider that this may be spirit asking you to develop more spiritually before doing this technique.

It is best to say an opening prayer for protection so that you are open to receiving guidance from the highest source. You may use this prayer or another that resonates with you:

"Creator, I call upon the protective forces in the universe to raise the vibration and provide communication from spirit through the flame. Only allow the highest and best energy and message to come through for me. Thank you."

Set your intention or ask your question. Sit and watch the flame, making sure you and your surroundings are safe and protected from anything that could burn. As you still and quiet your mind, be patient. Allow the energy to increase so that you can tap into the source of spirit working through the flame.

Singing around the bonfire can enhance your results by livening the energy and infusing the atmosphere with more joy and love. Gaze into the fire and watch as the flame changes color and shape. In some instances, you may find that the flame remains completely still and other times the flame is so active it nearly dances off the wick or wood (depending on which one you are using). You may ask your question and then concentrate on the flame. Just remain open to anything that comes. You can always ask the flame to respond to you in a question-and-answer format. For instance, ask the flame to move right for yes and move left for no. Then ask your questions and watch the flame shapeshift in front of you to produce answers.

The Jinn or Djinn are an ancient fire spirit and often appear in flames. They are supernatural, shape-shifting beings often associated with smokeless fire. The Jinn have free will much like humans do. They also possess remarkable powers and contact with them should not be taken lightly. If a supernatural being such as the Jinn appear to you through the fire, make sure you are respectful and use discernment. The Jinn can take whatever form they desire to and may appear as human, animal, or alien. We once captured on film an enormous hand with long talon fingers extending out from the fire. The grasp was aimed at only one person in our group and appeared in several photographs. The Jinn can often be thought of much in the same way as the fairies, as both can exhibit trickster energy. There is a long history of human contact with the Jinn and traditions from around the world validate their interactions.

Whenever you are doing something outside, the nature spirits may come to participate. This may include interactions with earth spirits such as gnomes or nature spirits such as fairies. Make sure you have proper discernment on who is communicating. While many nature, earth, and fire spirits can be tricksters, they can also be quite helpful. Especially if they view you as someone who values their way of life by caring for nature and the natural world they live in. Don't burn anything harmful in the fire (such as old tires or anything toxic to the environment) and burn only what you need. Always give thanks for any participation you receive.

If you attempt this process and don't get any results, be patient. They may want to become more familiar with you before they reveal themselves. The more you build trust and prove that you have pure intentions, the more nature, earth, and fire spirits will be inclined to help you.

We have had tremendous results while scrying into a bonfire and taking pictures. We have often captured both full and partial images in the fire with this technique. We once visited the Burlington Vortex and got consistently amazing pictures at a bonfire there; the images showed up only on film and not with the naked eye. The Burlington Vortex is located in Burlington, Wisconsin, and though it remains unmarked, guided tours are available through http://www.burlingtonnews.net/hauntedtours.html. As with any vortex site, the energy is increased, which is often a catalyst for supernatural phenomenon. The Burlington Vortex is particularly active with the Jinn, though this relationship may be established in any location through consistent visits and respect.

The use of a camera is also beneficial with this technique because the flame is quick to change and that may make it more difficult to discern images. Whether the images appear from spirit or Jinn, this technique should provide hours of interpretation and be useful to expand your awareness of the unseen world that exists around you.

When you have had a successful fire scrying session, make sure you complete the process by clearing your energy and silently closing the door to the spirit world. This can be done with a simple prayer or intention, such as:

"I give thanks to all who came to communicate with me and now close the door to the spirit world. Clear my aura of any residual energy and restore my own energy in my highest and best way now. Thank you." After reciting this clearing prayer, take a moment in silence with your eyes closed to feel the energy shift and clear around you.

Showing respect to the spirit world and natural world will help encourage future interactions.

Smoke Scrying

Capnomancy or smoke scrying is often associated with Native American cultures and Hoodoo, although it dates back to use in Babylonian times. This technique is similar to flame scrying but you will focus your intentions on the smoke. You may use any form of smoke, including smoke produced from burning incense or a fire. Some traditions add sacred herbs to the fire to enhance psychic vision. Tobacco, dragon's blood, jasmine, and myrrh are among the most favored. I enjoy using frankincense because it has such a high vibration that it adds to the element of protection as well. If you choose to use sacred herbs or incense, intend that this will create the protection and sacred space you desire.

Smoke scrying can be achieved by gazing into the smoke as you seek clarity, answers, or contact with the spirit world. The smoke will be similar to the cloud scrying in that it will move, shift, and often reveal images of spirit. It is easy for spirit to displace the smoke to create images that you may recognize as well as show you where they are. Nature spirits (fairies) may reveal themselves to you by allowing the smoke to penetrate the air surrounding them, leaving the air clear where they stand.

If you have a desire to connect with nature spirits, burn the incense near the item you would like to connect with. For instance, I have often taught people how to see fairies by burning incense around a living plant or flowers. The smoke will envelop the area, making subtle energy more visible. It is as if the smoke goes around the energetic body of the fairy, making it easier to detect. Once you see where those areas of clarity are, gently place your finger into the opening and see if you can feel a tingly sensation. Some of you may be able to see heat waves or sparkly lights above the aura of the plant. This may be a fairy or plant spirit.

Remember, those tiny fairies are quite powerful and love to play tricks on humans. Some people will have a natural ability to connect with them and will almost seem to attract fairies to them wherever they go. Fairies can be called upon for help with healing, learning how to garden more productively, or keeping predator animals from your yard. Typically, the fairies will require something in exchange. It is kind of an unwritten rule that they will take what they feel they deserve and not leave you the option of what the exchange will be. Although they do seem to like treats made of organic raw ingredients and especially dark chocolate (85 percent cocoa or higher). If you raise your vibration and connect with Creator before you make contact with fairies, they will not need to take anything in exchange for the help they provide.

Here is a suggested intention to say before you begin:

"Creator, I ask that you allow me to connect with the fairy and nature spirits in my highest and best way. I come with peace and respect for the nature world. Now show me."

Trust me when I say that I have done this the hard way too many times and had things go missing. There is nothing more frustrating than thinking you lost your car keys, cell phone, or jewelry. Fairies seem to especially like shiny little objects, though they can take just about anything. We have found that by asking them to return things and leaving them an offering, they will comply rather quickly. You can avoid exchange of give and take by just connecting to Creator energy before interacting.

As with the other techniques in this book, you may be able to capture the nature spirits with a digital camera. If you choose to do this, always ask permission of them before taking photos. They will have the option of appearing in the photo for you or not. So they don't feel an invasion of privacy, I always explain briefly that I share photos as a way to help educate people about their existence. Sometimes, you will find that they are very supportive of this effort and hope to gain the support from humans to save their environment.

If you prefer to connect with loved ones in spirit through smoke scrying, just change your intention. You may still use the camera if you choose as this method allows you to see what you may have missed with your physical eyes. With practice, you should increase your ability to see spirit with your physical eyes as well. In this case, you may set an intention as follows:

"Creator, I ask you to reveal my loved ones that are with me in spirit today. Please allow me to see and speak with them in the highest and best way for all concerned. Thank you."

Oil Scrying

Oil scrying is also known as lampadomancy and is a form of divination using a single oil lamp. The diviner interprets the movements of the flame to offer messages, just as with flame scrying. The history of oil scrying can be traced back to ancient Babylonian times. From there, it found its way to the Egyptians and Hebrews.

Another form of oil scrying is achieved when oil is carefully poured onto the surface of water. Fill a bowl with water for this exercise. Set your intention of what you wish to gain from the session and say a protection prayer:

"Creator, please allow me access to peer into the spirit world to connect with loved ones, angels, and guides. Only allow those to come through that have the highest and best intentions for me. Thank you."

When you feel ready, pour some oil onto the water. The water and oil do not mix and therefore create a unique pattern, which may be interpreted. Using oil on water for divination is called hydromancy. Any variation of the oil may be used. Some people prefer to use one type of oil over another. I will leave this up to you to explore and see which ones you get the best results with. Many people prefer to use sesame oil or olive oil but there really are no limits.

With oil scrying, you may also take photos if you wish. You may be surprised at how many images come through.

If it seems that no images are forming, restate your intention and give the oil and water mixture a little stir. Carefully watch as the shape continues to form images that could be interpreted by you. Remember, this is for you. Whatever you see is meant as a message for you and only you. If you are doing this exercise with another person, they may see something entirely different. Each person will see what is meant for them.

There are basically no limits to what you can use for scrying. The process induces a meditative state that allows the seeker to quiet their mind and connect to the spirit world around them.

In the next chapter, you will learn how to do the least-known form of scrying to develop your ability to see spirit. While mediumship scrying is fairly simple to learn, the results are astounding and will give you direct access to the spirit world.

four

Mediumship Scrying

In this chapter, you will learn how to mediumship scry in order to see spiritually. This technique is used for the purpose of seeing past lives, spirit guides, and deceased loved ones. You will need no special tools for this method to be effective, although it may take a little practice. It has been my experience that everyone can achieve results with this technique within a fairly short amount of time. The form of scrying presented here does not require complete sensory deprivation, although it does help to sit in a dimly lit room.

One of the first things that will appear during mediumship scrying is past life images of spirit. It is important to discuss past lives before we get started to prepare you for what you are about to encounter.

Some religions do not believe in past lives and you may find yourself wondering if you should believe in them or not. While it is not my objective to change your beliefs, I would like to share some information regarding the topic that may help you keep an open mind.

Some people believe that we absorb different personalities through group consciousness. Some believe that our soul is multidimensional and that it exists on multiple planes of existence at the same time. While no one really knows for sure, most agree that a soul is eternal: It exists before you come to earth and it exists after your physical body dies. Some believe that time is the ultimate illusion and that we are living all our lives—past, present, and future—simultaneously. When I refer to past lives in this book, allow the reference to encompass all of which I just mentioned or whatever piece that resonates with you most.

Whether past lives are as simple as once thought or more complex, they can be utilized as a powerful tool for healing. Many people with allergies, fears, phobias, and some health problems have been healed instantly when they approached healing a trauma created in a previous lifetime. It may not matter if past lives are successive or happening all at once, there is still much to learn from all of them.

Children seem to be particularly open to the experiences of past lifetimes and often recall memories of when they were someone else. When a young child begins to discuss who they were before this life or who you were to them, it can be unsettling at first. Many of these children are actually recalling their names, important historical events, and verifiable facts about the lives they once lived. This experience often startles parents who may not know how to handle it or advise the child. In some cases, these children were born with the agenda to heal things that were left undone from their last existence. It is also possible that they are connected to the memories of another soul and believe that those experiences were their own. When parents gently allow the child to work through the unhealed issues, the memories seem to fade and more focus on the current life prevails. These memories seem to be the strongest between the ages of one and five years old.

When my daughter was three, she insisted that I was her sister and would introduce me as such. Time and time again, I would correct her by telling her that I was her mommy. It wasn't until years later when multiple psychics confirmed we were twin sisters in a previous life that I began to consider it. Due to my upbringing in a traditional religious family, I wasn't educated or open minded about past lives yet. I have since determined that something very real exists before our current reality and I have accepted the possibility of past lives. In my daughter's case, she didn't have any particular trauma to work through; she just seemed content to have another opportunity to be with me and an awareness that this wasn't the first time or place that we met.

In the healing work I do with clients, I often discover patterns of behavior or suffering that were established before my client was born. Sometimes I find that they inherited certain memories and patterns from their genetic family, even when they never met their ancestors. Other times, I see visions of who they were in the past and the events surrounding their death, which caused patterns of illness or suffering in this life. I have also become aware that some people who cannot accept a healing in the here and now are often more amenable to accepting it at a different point in their timeline. This simply means that whether or not a memory of a past life is factual, it is still possible to do healing at that point in time and receive the benefit of the healing in the here and now.

In working with past lives, my goal is always aimed at healing in the current life. While it can be mesmerizing to get caught up in the possibility of all your previous lifetimes, consider that we are here now to live the fullest life possible. If exploring your past lives helps to heal issues that you currently have, then it may be a viable process for you to explore. I caution against getting so caught up in other realities that you forget who you are now and neglect to really be present in your current life.

Embarking on past lives can be quite empowering and can help offer answers to many questions you may have about yourself. If you have always had a fear of water and there are no tragic events surrounding water in this life, perhaps it was created in a previous one. Discovering an unhealed issue and resolving it can bring tremendous healing to your life now.

Another thing you may want to consider is the ability to bring forth any amazing talents that you acquired while living previously. Suppose you worked very hard to learn a specific skill in a previous life. Can you tap into that skill and bring it forward to your current life? Yes, you can! If your soul is infinite and we are all that we ever were before, then it is possible to access those parts of yourself that you previously mastered.

As you begin to scry, you will see many faces. These first images are typically going to be what we refer to as past life personalities. If you are sitting with a partner, you will see all that they once were. You may notice that a person who has a particularly masculine energy may have had the majority of their past life experiences as a male. If you see many youthful faces upon your partner, it means that their soul has not yet experienced old age or the benefits of gaining wisdom through experience. They may tend to be childlike in their approach to life. On the other hand, you may see that the person you sit with exposes many wrinkled faces filled with ancient knowledge. This indicates that the person would have reached old age many times and their soul would have gained much from those lengthy times on earth. Seeing all of who a person is can give you quite a lot of insights into who they are now.

As you move forward with scrying, keep an open mind. If your view of past lives differs from what is presented here, that's okay. You will definitely still see faces and images of other personalities and/or lifetimes. However you choose to interpret the images is up to you. Just remember to keep an open mind, and release all judgment about what you may see next.

Mediumship Scrying Exercise

Here is what you will need to get started. Scrying may be done at the kitchen table or in a private sitting room, whichever you prefer. There should be a table between two chairs with a candle in the middle. The room should be dark, but complete darkness is not required. You may want to set a timer to ensure you allow yourself enough time for the process to work. Initially, it is best to go for longer durations until you become adept at seeing spirit and subtle energy. With practice, you may see spirit faces immediately and will not need to set a timer at all. However, as you begin using this technique, it is best to allow up to twenty minutes for each sitting.

You will do this exercise with another person, so choose a trusted friend or loved one. It is not necessary that you believe in spirits or have any previous experience as long as you approach scrying with an open mind. Both sitters should do a short meditation to clear their energy before they begin. This could be as simple as breathing a few times to relax. Close your eyes and inhale with the intention of bringing in clear energy to help connect with spirit. Exhale with the intention of residual energy from the day being lifted and sent to the heavens. Allow any fear, worry, or projected outcomes to be lifted away so that clarity can take its place. Do this a few times as you prepare to scry.

Light the candle and set it between the two people who will be scrying together. It should be about a foot away from each person's face so that they receive equal amounts of illumination from the flame. Be sure that there are no breezes if you are sitting outside or that you are not sitting by an air vent or fan as this will cause the flame to flicker and may disrupt the energy, sometimes causing false results.

As with any form of spirit work, it is always recommended to say a prayer of protection or to set the intention of only allowing what is your highest and best to come through. Imagine a protective shell surrounding both people in a bubble of light. Any prayer will do, so use the one you feel most comfortable with. Here is a sample protection prayer:

"Creator, it is commanded to call upon my angels and guides to assist me with the process of scrying and to illuminate the room with a bubble of protection and unconditional love. I set my intention to witness and connect with spirit and to use this process with integrity and for the highest and best for all. Thank you."

Now you may begin to send energy to your partner through your third eye. Imagine that a beam of light is emerging from your forehead and going to your partner as they are also sending the energy and light back to your third eye. You may focus your eyes on the bridge of the nose or look directly into your partner's eyes. It is very important that the energy is not interrupted by talking or laughing during the session. You may, of course, blink. But otherwise, be prepared to sit in silence and concentrate your energy on seeing your partner's past lives.

When the faces begin to emerge, it is most common to see a fading out of your partner's face. The eyes generally stay the same while the rest of the face continues to change as new features begin to emerge. Consider yourself a passive moviegoer at this point. Don't try to analyze what you see, just allow the show of faces to continue. You will find that when you are free of expectations, you will be able to perceive much more. The more you do this, the more clairvoyant you will become. This will enable you to intuitively feel and know things about the images you see. You may pick up on the personalities of the individuals, as well as how they lived and died. If you do this process and only see the faces without gaining insight into any additional information, consider it a success. The rest will come with practice.

You may find that your eyes get weary and may feel dry or produce tears. Again, it is okay to blink when this happens. However, be aware that if you can look for just a moment longer, you may be on the verge of seeing spiritually. Oftentimes, blinking helps to moisten the eyes but it also resets the vision. If you have ever looked into a 3-D picture you may already be familiar with the process of allowing your vision to go out of focus slightly. If not, that may be another tool you could use to help you develop your skills faster. People who see into the spiritual dimensions are usually using a soft focus with their sight. That means that you don't allow your eyes to constantly focus in on any one item but instead allow the peripheral to expand. Allow things to go a little blurry and trust in the process.

Most of the time, the images you see first will look as though your partner's own face has changed. If you are not prepared for this, it can be startling at first. You will notice that the eyes remain unchanged even as the rest of the features shift and turn into other people. The eyes truly are the window to the soul and have recorded every moment from every lifetime that they have experienced. As you keep a soft focus on the eyes, allow your peripheral vision to release the present image and produce the past images for you. The size and shape of the face will change, bringing forward many human faces along with some unfamiliar images that may be considered alien or animal. The hairstyles will change as well as the age and gender. You may notice some identifier items such as eyeglasses, feather headdresses, hats, armor, and different-era attire. Pay attention to any scars shown on the face too.

As you do this, you are peering into the timeless existence of your partner's soul. Wait until the timer goes off before you share details or you will lose your link and the energy will fade. It is okay if you cannot immediately recall all of the images when the session ends. Sometimes they appear so fast in secession that if you focus on trying to remember them; you will miss the next ones. Just relax and allow yourself to witness the spirit display. Your mind will remember all the images that it saw and can be recalled if you take a moment to close your eyes and call upon them after the session is done.

If at any time, you see an image change emotions, turn their head, or smile, it means you have made contact with a spirit. Typically, the order in which the faces will emerge will be past life faces first, spirit guides or ghosts, and then deceased loved ones. Don't be discouraged if it takes you a while to see deceased loved ones. Everything is a process and they will appear to you when you are ready to see them. This technique will help you get there.

Loved ones in spirit will typically show up beside the face of the sitter. I have also seen them hovering slightly above the sitter, and at times superimposed in front of them. The spirit world is very organized, so if you are unsure if you saw a spirit or a past life image, simply ask the spirit to take position. Grandparents, parents, and siblings will be very close to the sitter's face. The paternal side of the family will often appear to the right of the sitter while the left is considered the maternal side. Lovers, friends, and associates will often show up slightly farther away from the sitter's face to indicate they are not a blood relative, and they also tend to show up on the maternal left side of the sitter.

Once you are able to do this technique with success, the process will speed up dramatically. At this point, you will be able to open your intuitive abilities to the next level. When you encounter an image more than once, this is an indication that the past life has a recurring issue that needs to be healed in the here and now. This may also indicate that there is healing needed for the spirit of the recurring past personality. Yes, it is possible for parts of your soul to remain unhealed even as the rest of your soul has moved on to future lifetimes. Send healing, forgiveness, and release to any part of you/your partner that may need it. You may purposefully go back into the meditative state of scrying with your partner and intuitively ask the past life personality questions. Do not speak out loud, ask the questions in your mind. You will intuitively receive the answers through a feeling or knowing.

When you are finished, take turns sharing what you saw and sensed as well as any answers that you received from spirit. Always give thanks to spirit for participating and then clear your energy. This is best done by closing your eyes and mentally bringing all your energy back to yourself and visualizing that you are disconnected from your partner and from spirit. You may call in angels to clear your energy field, wash off in white light, or any other practice that you are accustomed to. You may also use the edge of your hand to physically cut the air between you and your partner to help this process.

The cleansing portion of this technique is very important and should not be overlooked. In a way, you are opening a portal to the spirit world and this portal should be closed at the end of each session. This does not mean that you are blocking any loved ones from making further contact. It only means that you are closing the doorway to disallow any other forms of spirit to attempt coming through. Your loved ones in spirit are always around you and they will continue to be able to contact you as before, often through a touch, a dream, or whatever way you have felt comforted by their presence. If you have not felt the presence of your loved ones in spirit prior to this exercise, you may begin to.

You may use the following prayer or say any prayer or intention that resonates with you:

"Thank you for working with my energy to allow me to see and witness spirit for the highest good. I close the door to the spirit world with gratitude and love. Shower me off with Creator's light, cleansing off any spiritual debris and restoring my energy field. Cleanse this space of any residual energy as well and purify it with unconditional love and Creator's light. Thank you."

The more you work with the mediumship scrying technique, the better prepared you will be for transfiguration. If you find that you are getting consistent results and that this technique works well for you, it is time for you to advance to transfiguration.

Personal Scrying Experiences

Alien Face

The technique of scrying may also be performed in a group setting. In a group, one person sits holding a candle just under their face. The group arranges itself in a semicircle formation so they can all view the person to scry upon. The first time I did this exercise, there were approximately twenty people gathered and we all took turns sitting for the group. The same rules apply as the room should be dimly lit and silent. I was in position a little over halfway around the circle and commenced scrying upon a classmate who was a friend of mine. Her face began to shift and change very quickly, and then I noticed one particular image really take hold as it lingered far longer than the others. The image was definitely some sort of alien face with greenish-blue skin full of pits and bumps. There appeared to be two tall protrusions in place of horns or antennae. The eyes are what stood out the most, because although the face was odd-colored and textured, the eyes emanated a gentle all-knowingness with deep compassion for earth. I got the impression that this was an ancient creature who had been in existence for a very long time.

There was no time to doubt what I saw because two other sitters also described seeing the exact same image. I did not feel that this image was a typical past life face that would have transmitted during scrying, but instead was some sort of alien spirit, or perhaps an alien spirit guide.

My friend, who was holding the candle, laughed and made light about what we saw as she did not believe in aliens at that time. She came from a traditional and grounded background, having retired from the police force. I sketched the face I saw on a little piece of paper to represent the image I had seen. Months later, my friend told me that, while she initially thought we were crazy, she no longer doubted what we had seen. She had begun to have some experiences of her own that she could only describe as coming from another dimension or life form.

She was having dreams and spirit visitations accompanied by symbols in light surrounding her bed. In one encounter, she described what seemed to be a transmission of ancient knowledge. Though she didn't understand the symbols or content of what was given to her, she felt that the experience was beneficial and that it was somehow enhancing her spiritual development. Because our soul is infinite, it is possible to comprehend and absorb ancient teachings in the form of light, vibration, and sound without our current personality grasping the meaning. Rest assured, if this happens, the soul will upgrade your personality with the knowledge when you are most able to accept new ideas of thought.

The experiences my friend began to have changed her outlook and shifted her perspective about life in many ways. I believe that the alien we saw while scrying had already been trying to work with her because it was already present in her energy field. It gave us great comfort to have seen the alien and looked into its eyes to know the depth of compassion and love that it felt for humanity.

We laugh now when we see my little sketch of the alien face, and we truly believe it to be one of her spirit guides that work through her. She has since taken up healing and continues to learn and grow through many techniques and disciplines. Many of her healing methods seem to come from within her own imagination or inner guidance. Perhaps this is the effect of some alien downloads she received or perhaps her soul was awakened through this experience. Regardless, she has had to confront some of her fears and beliefs about aliens and non-human life forms as she began to accept this presence in her life. Without a doubt, she has become much more open-minded from this experience.

Lyrian = Cat People

The first time I sat to scry with my daughter, I saw some unusual images. At the time, I didn't have any frame of reference for what I was seeing. Her mildly curly hair sprang into tighter curls around her face as furry ears emerged from the top of her head. I literally saw cat-like whiskers and a flat, triangle-shaped nose. Some of her other features remained the same as if she had only turned into a cat halfway. I blinked and suggested we start again to refresh my vision. But time and time again, I saw what looked to be cat people. Half human and half cat.

My daughter has always had a great love for animals but particularly cats. All she ever wanted when she was little was a cat. We had always rented houses and apartments that would not allow cats, so she was nine years old before I finally agreed to sneak one into our rental. The house we were living in had no carpet so I figured it could not do any damage. She loved her cat immensely and seemed to have a real understanding of him. In return, our male tabby thought of her as his litter mate rather than a pet owner. Many years later, we adopted another male cat who also accepted her as a litter mate—sharing a close bond of security and safety with her. Both cats slept in her bed and one didn't leave her side.

It was no surprise that each time someone sat to scry with my daughter the first thing they saw was a cat person. It got to be a joke, because without knowing any previous details about her or her personality, they would ask in disbelief, "Did she just turn into a cat person?"

I have scryed with my daughter many times over the years and every time I have seen at least one cat person. Often, I see many images of different cat people, as if those are the previous lifetimes that she has had. While it may seem highly impossible to have had lifetimes as a cat person, I am reminded by my late mentor Alan, who said, "We didn't all originate on planet earth." Without further judgment, I have learned to accept what I get when I scry and try to do my best to eliminate any prejudices about what I see.

While sharing this experience with a healer who is a friend of mine, she didn't blink twice in reference to the oddity about cat people. In fact, she didn't think it odd at all. She told me about the Lyrian (Cat People) race and told me to look up information about them. The Lyrian are a star race of cat people that have been interacting with humans for the evolution of mankind.

I am not suggesting that my daughter is Lyrian, but she may be influenced by the Lyrian energy in ways that I do not yet understand. Or perhaps, her experience is similar to my friend with the greenish-blue alien that works with her as a spirit guide.

It is best to scry with an open mind and try not to analyze every facet of what you see. You will be amazed and may find similar images with the people you choose to scry with. It would be interesting to see if all cat lovers have this image in common while scrying. If you are a cat lover, see if you have this image appear as well.

Temple Prostitute and Spontaneous Scrying

While attending classes for Intuitive Anatomy, I uncovered many hidden subconscious beliefs that I carried from past lifetimes. The process we use to discover them is called muscle testing. There are multiple ways to muscle test, which simply means testing the strength of your muscles. "Yes" responses by the body will generate a strong or firm muscle, while "No" responses cause a weakened state.

The most common forms of muscle testing are standing, using one arm outstretched or a grip between the ring finger and thumb. The easiest to demonstrate here is the standing test. Face north and stand with your feet shoulder-width apart and your arms down at your sides. Close your eyes and say out loud "yes." If you are properly hydrated, your body should want to pull slightly forward. Stand straight up again and say out loud "no." At this time, you should feel your body slightly move backward. Once your body is testing accurately for yes and no, you may make statements to navigate your subconscious beliefs.

Keep in mind that the subconscious holds many beliefs and they may not resonate with your conscious mind at all. In other words, the subconscious mind often holds the secrets to what it is we really need to heal. We can access past life beliefs, ancestral beliefs, and group consciousness beliefs that we accepted as ours.

In the class, once we found out what beliefs were affecting us or holding us back from healing, we learned how to clear them from all places in time. Clearing old beliefs meant that we were no longer affected by old beliefs from previous lifetimes and they no longer interfered with our current life. During class, I unearthed some strange beliefs and didn't know where they originated from. Were they ancestral, past life, or group consciousness beliefs?

My instructor informed me that I had certain beliefs carried over that were consistent with being a temple prostitute. I had never heard that term before, but when I looked into the meaning it felt as if the very cells in my body responded with affirmation.

According to ancient Greek historian Herodotus, there was a Babylonian custom that required women to sit in the temple of Aphrodite until being selected by a stranger for the act of sacred sex; this happened at least once in the woman's lifetime. Temple prostitutes often worked out of shrines or temples, some of which were referred to as houses of heaven. In other ancient cultures, the temple prostitute was a person who had sacred sex for the purpose of bringing others closer to God. In some cultures, she was raised to the status of high priestess and would be offered to kings and the ruling elite. Sacred sex was often part of fertility rituals or divine marriage in other cultures.

After class, I went to visit a close friend of mine and was sharing the strange insights I had gained in class regarding temple prostitutes. We discussed the ancient beliefs that I somehow had carried into this lifetime and that I was able to change them. As I was telling her about the history, my friend listened intently and then remarked that she may have similar beliefs from earlier lifetimes as well. We had met in a spiritual development class years earlier and had an instant rapport. Our friendship was characterized by a sisterhood of sorts, an instant, close bond. We often wondered if we knew each other from a different lifetime. Suddenly, something clicked and we began to muscle test her to see if she also had temple prostitute beliefs. It shouldn't have been such a surprise when we discovered that she did. Perhaps that was the lifetime when we first met and began our friendship.

When it was time to leave, my friend walked me out to my car and we stood talking for a little while longer under her yard light. I became transfixed on her image as she began to spontaneously change forms right in front of my eyes. She appeared to be about four inches shorter than her current stature and the shape of her head and face changed. Her hair became curly and was worn up in a loose bun while the features on her face were markedly different. I remember studying her nose carefully as she talked and it became clear that this was no longer the physical embodiment of my friend as I knew her in this life. We lingered in discussion as we said goodbye, mostly because I wanted to see who this spirit was that was showing herself to me. I didn't say a word about the changes I saw and when we finally parted, I drove home thinking about it the whole way.

The following morning, my friend called me very early. She just couldn't refrain from sharing what she had witnessed the night before. She said that something really strange had happened while we were visiting and it kept her up all night. She was so freaked out at first that she didn't want to say anything but finally felt compelled to tell me. She began to disclose that as we were standing in the yard, talking under the light, that my face changed and I appeared as someone completely different. I gasped and shared with her that I had also had the same experience at the exact same time!

This is a case of spontaneous scrying. You should expect this to happen as you become adept at scrying and seeing subtle changes in energy and spirit. However, this was also a simultaneous scrying incident, which can happen when two people are spiritually connected or on the same wavelength or frequency as each other. My friend is a spiritual person who is both open-minded and adept at scrying. While I have spontaneously scryed and have seen people change before my eyes, and my students have claimed to see me shift and change into other people when I am teaching, this was the only instance of spontaneous and simultaneous scrying that I can recall to date. I believe it may be due to the conversation we were having and the possible past life connection we had.

Perhaps we were both open-minded enough to see who we once were when we began our friendship and similar life experiences in another time and place. The experience lasted for several consecutive minutes and the changes were physical, where we each embodied a different person. This experience is quite rare but is possible. I cannot say with certainty that either of us actually had a past life as a temple prostitute, but I can say that what we experienced that night will forever intrigue me.

Grief Demon

Most of the time, scrying will reveal past lifetimes. However, it can also alert you to any spirits or entities that are hanging around a person.

I was teaching a class on scrying when one of my students commented that she saw a menacing creature every time she looked at her partner. I decided to switch the students around and allow her to work with a different partner. At first, the scrying session went as normal, but then she also saw the same creature on the new partner. At times, it is possible for someone to see an entity on other people when it is really attached to them and exists in their energy field or aura.

I decided to intervene and sat to scry with my student. As we began the process, I detected the entity that my student had reported seeing on other classmates. It was indeed attached to her and was somewhat stuck in her energy field. This was not a past life image but rather a troublesome, lower entity that was hovering around in my student's aura. With my background working with the spirit world, I was able to easily clear the entity for my student without fear or drama.

I inquired if my student had been aware of the entity's presence prior to class. She confessed that she had felt a dark energy around her lately and that it was draining her energy and making her feel angry and depressed. I asked her if she could detect when she first began to feel that way to ascertain when and how she allowed this spirit to attach to her. After a brief moment of thought, she knew immediately when the attachment occurred. About a month prior to class, she had lost one of her parents and was in the process of grieving. She decided to take a walk in nature to try to clear her head. She walked in an area unfamiliar to her and recalled sitting down on a bench and weeping. She was alone in the woods and could remember the stillness all around her. She also remembered feeling angry about her loss and fearful about her future. Both are typical feelings that one feels as they grieve and they typically pass with time. She said that she hadn't felt the same since that moment.

Entities are opportunistic. They can often find openings to a person who is feeling emotionally weak. This typically happens when a person is engaged with drugs or alcohol but may happen at especially difficult times in a person's life when their vibration is lower than normal. Thankfully, my student was not afraid of the entity and did not refuse to allow us to scry after the initial discovery of it. She was happy to have it sent away and felt her emotional state elevate when it was gone. You will find a clearing technique in chapter 8; use it whenever you come across a negative spirit.

It is important to have no fear when doing any kind of spiritual work. All kinds of spiritual energies are around us at all times. If you encounter something not of the light, know that you have authority to send it away. I'm going to reaffirm the importance of protection and clearing with any kind of spiritual work. But also, in your normal daily life. We are spiritual beings inhabiting a physical body and as spiritual beings ourselves, we are subjected to many different forms of energy every single day of our life through all our experiences, places we visit, and people we see. In fact, we are subjected to thought forms from others, knowingly and unknowingly.

There are so many things that affect our energy and it is up to us to keep a clear energy field. The best advice is to make protection a morning ritual and to make clearing a part of your nightly routine. Regardless if you participate in scrying, energy work, or mediumship, clearing your energy should be a daily routine for every living being. Animals are included in this, too, as they often clear their beloved masters of negative debris in an effort to help them heal.

Visit from Mummy

It was a beautiful summer afternoon and we had invited friends from our paranormal group out to visit. Our friends were a married couple that had established the paranormal group and ran it successfully for longer than any other group in the Twin Cities. We first met in 2004 when they investigated the most noted haunted house I had lived in. We quickly became friends and I eventually joined their team of paranormal investigators. Every time we got together, we enjoyed sharing new devices and techniques for communicating with the spirit world.

On a previous visit, I showed the husband how to scry. He had many gifts for mediumship and was experienced in the field of parapsychology. However, he had never seen anything like what I was about to show him. As we began to scry, he doubted that he would be able to see anything and our session was unsuccessful. We cut the first session short, refocused, and then began again. A few minutes into the procedure, he belted out a squeamish little girl scream that shocked us all. He was overcome with hysterical laughter until he literally fell off his chair and onto the floor, still belly laughing.

I was shocked at his genuine surprise and couldn't wait to find out what he had seen. When he finally emerged from his laughter, he explained that while he still doubted he would be able to see anything, my face changed right before his eyes! He said that he witnessed my face transform into a very old woman with deeply weathered and wrinkled skin. At one moment, he was gazing upon my face and then suddenly, an ancient woman was staring back at him. He was tremendously pleased that he was able to see her with his own eyes and I quickly identified her as a face that many others had seen with me before.

His wife was eager to learn this technique and have the opportunity to scry with us. She was from England where she worked on haunted castle tours. I hoped she would be open to the experience of scrying and couldn't wait to get started. I explained the technique to her as we lit the candle and said our prayer for protection.

The moment we opened our eyes and began to scry, I immediately saw the image of a woman in spirit beside her. The female spirit shared some similar features with my friend but she appeared slightly older, with shoulder-length dark brown hair. I estimated that she was in her late forties and intuitively felt that she was her mother. Her spirit was actually positioned right over the left shoulder of my friend, so if this was her mother, she was in the correct position. However, I didn't know anything about her family or if her mother had even passed. I could not continue to scry after seeing the spirit so clearly and felt compelled to share what I had seen.

My friend immediately began to cry because she was able to validate the description I gave her as her mummy who had passed. Her mummy had died in her late forties and she had dark brown hair, wore it shoulder length, and looked similar to my friend, with some facial features in common. My friend said that she had been to many mediums to try to connect with her mummy but no one had been able to make contact with her.

I was thrilled that her mum had decided to join us and understood now why she jumped into our session right away. Once a connection is established between spirit and the living, it is easy to go back to connect for further communication. I was able to connect with her mum and help bring healing and closure to some unresolved issues. Spirits are on their toes. This means that they often know who you are going to see and what you are going to do before you do. This was not the first time I have experienced spirit's hand in arranging meetings and events.

My friend's mother knew that they were coming for a visit and came along, knowing that we were planning to scry. She chose that opportunity to come through to reconnect with her daughter and to let her know that she was doing well on the other side. It was a beautiful surprise for me too. Thanks, mummy!

Spirit with Bun and Pearls

My family was having dinner at a friend's house when we decided to share the scrying technique with them. I was positioned across the kitchen table from my girlfriend and we were deeply entranced in our scrying session. My husband stood still as he took photos of us. We had discovered that previous life images could sometimes be captured in photographs so we often took photos while scrying. It seemed best to stand in one stationary position while capturing pictures from the side angle. A tripod works best for holding a position and ensures that the camera is not moved while capturing photos.

We proceeded to scry while my husband took approximately forty pictures with a digital camera. Upon reviewing the photographs, we noticed many images protruding in front of our own faces, as we had often experienced before. Some faces we recognized as ones we had seen while scrying and others were new to us. Perhaps they appeared too quickly for our eyes to detect. However, on one of the photos, there was an image of a woman superimposed over my friend's head. This was not the normal position for past life faces to appear so we spent extra time examining the photograph. Much to our surprise, we could clearly make out the spirit woman's features. While my friend was scrying, facing me at a profile, the spirit woman was looking directly at the camera as if she was completely aware that her photo was being taken. She appears to have dark hair worn in a high bun with a big smile on her face. She is wearing a pearl necklace and feels to be from an earlier era, perhaps the 1940s. We could see the image so clearly that we thought our friend must have known the woman, perhaps it was a deceased relative. However, upon examination of the photo, she could not identify the spirit woman.

This photo remains one of our favorite spirit photos, clearly demonstrating that spirits do show up for scrying sessions. This was also an added reminder to clear the space before and after a scrying session. We thanked the spirit woman for showing up and concluded that our friend must have gotten an attachment earlier in the day.

Most attachments are not harmful, as spirits are especially drawn to mediums and healers. But it is important to note that if the spirits are attaching to you and following you home, they are doing so for a reason. It may be beneficial to learn how to cross over spirits if you have this happen to you often. Most of the time, the spirits around you will be loved ones that have already crossed over and are by your side to assist you. But when a ghost attaches itself to you, it will be an unfamiliar spirit who most likely needs a little assistance in finding their way into the light. This type of stowaway can follow you home and drain your energy, sometimes causing sickness or chaos until they are released. (See "Clear Space Exercise" in chapter 8.)

Mustache Man

My husband and I decided to spend the evening scrying with our teenage daughters. We were sitting poolside on a hot and humid night, gazing over a single candle and taking photos of our scrying session. This was early on in our scrying days and we were all excited to see what we could photograph and experience. One of the things that made scrying so much fun was that it was easy to teach. And to this day, I have not encountered anyone that could not do it with a little practice.

My husband was halfway into a scrying session with our daughter when I noticed the photographs were showing amazing results. One of the strange phenomena that occurs during scrying is that the lights became like liquid. If there is a candle in the room, it would appear like a streak of light running the entire frame of the picture. If there were light bulbs on, they, too, would become like liquid streaks, even when the lights were outside or next door. This indicates that the energy produced through scrying does not merely raise the energy between the two participating in the session but that it has a much broader effect on the immediate surroundings. The moment the scrying session is complete, the energy returns to normal. Lights that were liquid-like are returned to normal too. All blurry images return to clear in subsequent photos.

During this particular scrying session, we noticed a dramatic male face positioned in front of our daughter's face. He had a strong nose and bushy eyebrows, dark brown hair, and a very obvious old-fashioned mustache that grew into his hairline. He also seemed to impress physical changes upon our daughter's arm. While her arm was very slender, in the photograph it appears to be well-developed and muscular. We were so focused on the spirit man's face that we didn't notice the muscular arm until we had studied the photo for quite a while.

This was one of the first scrying sessions that we photographed, and the photo was reviewed by my mentor, Alan Arcieri. He was impressed that we were able to capture a spirit image so clearly, and concluded that it was an authentic spirit photograph. We had taken the pictures merely to remember a family moment rather than for a means of capturing evidence. It was this photo that taught us that this process was a viable way to capture proof of spirit and perhaps we were guided to it. As it turned out, it has proven to consistently work as a means of capturing spirit images. This photo remains one our favorite ghost photos to this day.

Spirit Guides

In terms of scrying photographs, we always learn something new. Spirit is always teaching us something and the scrying technique has been a consistent method for expanding our awareness of spirit.

One night, our children were scrying and my husband and I were taking turns photographing them. They were excited to see the results and laughed each time they saw their sibling's face change. It was a fun experiment, but in the atmosphere of laughing and talking we could not produce any spirit images on the camera. Finally, we told the kids to really focus their energy with no talking. We set the timer to make sure they knew that a small window of silent time would soon come to an end and they could burst out in laughter and discussion at that time.

On the second attempt, the kids really put their all into it and focused their energy toward one another. The room was so silent that even the onlookers were prompted to stillness. The energy in the entire room was extremely high and felt dramatically different than it did moments before. We looked on as the scrying continued and my husband took many photos with a digital camera.

When we reviewed the photographs that time, we noticed something we had never seen before or since. We captured a photograph of our daughters scrying with each other, but it looks as if there are four people in the photo instead of two. Upon closer examination, the two images, closest to the candle and in the center of the photograph are the images of our daughters how we know them and see them. There are two other images farther away from the candle and on the outer perimeter of the photograph that appear slightly different than each daughter. This photo is perplexing in that there is no rational explanation to debunk it. If the camera had moved while taking the photo, for instance, any additional images would have appeared in the direction that the camera moved. However, the two (extra) images that appeared were on the outside of each daughter, both being on the perimeter of the photo on opposite sides. There was no way to duplicate the results, though we tried.

Due to the position and uniqueness of the photo, we believe we may have captured our daughters' spirit guides. Typically, the past life images will appear in front of the face. Spirits and ghosts may appear in any area; superimposed over the head, in front of the person, or to the side. In this particular photo, we have two different images appearing very clearly behind each of our daughters while they were in deep concentration. Could it be images of a past life? It's possible. Could it be ancestor spirits? That's possible too. Whatever it is, we are still learning from it and continue to be fascinated by the photo.

Texas Rancher

Many years ago, I signed up to attend a spirit gathering at the local spiritual center that I frequented. It was to be held by a reputable medium who had a long-standing practice in the area. She was a very good friend of mine and I loved to attend classes and meditations that she led. There were about twenty people gathered and we sat in a large circle with multiple candles lit in the center. The medium went into meditation and began to raise her energy. All the participants were eager to see what happened. The candlelight began to dance, high and then low with a little wiggle of the flame from time to time. We held the intention of connecting to our own loved ones in spirit. I'm not sure what we expected to experience, but it seemed that everyone was getting impatient with the process.

At this point, the medium decided to channel to see who she could connect with in the spirit world. The room fell silent and the energy began to build again. First, the medium began to speak in a deep male voice accompanied by a western drawl. When I glanced up to look at her, I clearly saw the face of the spirit man that she was channeling. He was talking about his cattle in Texas and seemed a little confused as to how he got to our circle. This was a first for me, so I looked around eagerly, anticipating that everyone else could see him too. (I had to prove I wasn't crazy or seeing things, after all!) But no one else reacted to the visual manifestation.

Suddenly, his conversation was interrupted by another spirit who spoke in a softer tone with an English accent. I noticed at this time that an old woman appeared, hovering over the face of the medium. Although I had experienced seeing spirits while scrying, I had not heard (or seen) one channeled before. I had never even experienced a channeling until that night. This time, I looked around the group to see if anyone else could see the older woman and caught the surprised expression upon another student's face. She was seated about halfway around the circle from me and we both looked at each other with confirmation. Yes, we both could see the spirit faces emerging upon the medium as she channeled them.

Although many of the other students did not experience what I had seen, it was a real treat to know that it was witnessed by another person. The other student who saw the spirit faces had also become adept at scrying. I have to give credit where credit is due. The scrying technique helped me to see spirit with my physical eyes. It was also fun to be able to validate that the medium truly was channeling the spirits she claimed to be connected to; we saw them as clearly as if they had physically entered the room!

Divine Teaching

There is a strange phenomenon that happens when I teach. My students have been telling me this for years. When I am teaching and really feel connected to the information I am talking about, my face changes.

The first time I became aware of this phenomenon was actually during a healing session with a client. Most of the time when I work with clients in person, they close their eyes and relax. This client could not do that, because she was deaf and had to keep her eyes open. A big part of the healing session requires that I get verbal consent for each portion of the healing and different changes that we make. Without being able to hear me, this client would not be able to give consent without reading my lips.

It was toward the end of our session and I had just finished with a rather large combination of clearing and feeling work when I slowly opened my eyes. Typically at this point in a session, when my eyes open I cannot see clearly what is in front of me. It is as if I am seeing through a window or veil and it takes a moment to come back into the space of this reality. After a few seconds, my eyes begin to see physically again and I can anchor into the room by noting the surroundings and my client's face. In this case, it is difficult to accurately describe the look upon my client's face in the moment when I became anchored again. Her eyes and mouth were wide open with a combined look of shock and bewilderment. I thought for a moment that I had done something and asked what was wrong. Had I spaced out and left her sitting for too long without communication? Had I disappeared from sight, which is how I felt when deeply entranced? I didn't know what to think of her reaction until I asked.

She then told me that she had witnessed my face change, stretch outward and upward, and then come back in the form of someone else, many times while I was administering the healing. I didn't know what to think of it at the time and thought perhaps it was a one-time occurrence, or that perhaps it was my client's ability to see spirit that made this situation possible. However, over the years since that time, my students have all shared that they have witnessed me changing into other people as I teach.

The classes I teach are all about healing, working with spirit, and mediumship development. I know the material well, but there are times when I feel like another energy moves into me to teach it from the highest truth. It is at those times that I feel most connected to Creator and know that what I am teaching is meant to be here on earth. Many teachers may know what I am talking about when I describe it as a divine teaching. The energy is just right, the information is at its purest, and the students are most receptive. It's almost as if liquid light is replacing my very words as we are pulled into a higher vibration.

At some point, I would like to be photographed while teaching class so I can witness the phenomenon for myself. Until then, I'll count on my students to let me know when it happens. They always do!

Tale of Two Healers

One of the things I have noticed is that scrying can take on even more phenomenal results if the two participants are skilled at working with energy. We did an experiment at my house when I was being visited by another healer. She was also trained as a ThetaHealer, so we both knew how to slow our brain waves down and raise our vibration through connecting with Creator energy, and setting our intention and focus on connecting to the highest light. I had never thought to apply the technique of ThetaHealing to this technique of scrying because it worked so well on its own. But in the spirit of exploration, we decided to see if our energy could be amplified even more by combining the techniques. We were hoping to increase our results and, as it turned out, we were right. The experiment proved to be a success and the photographs were unlike any others we had taken in the past.

We were seated on either side of a small round table with a single candle in the center. Our arms were rested comfortably on top of the table during the session. We both sent our energy up to connect with the Creator and requested that our energy be raised to assist us with the scrying session. Then, as we opened our eyes, we commenced scrying as usual by sending energy to each other through our third eye.

This dynamic was so powerful and intense that we captured photos unlike any that were taken before. Of course, we still captured images of spirit faces in front of our own, but we also captured things that we had never seen before. In some photos, the table that we had our arms resting on literally looked to be hovering above our heads. The only thing that I can compare this to is called a dimension shift that frequently occurs at vortex sites. It takes a tremendous amount of energy to shift the surroundings in this way. In many of the photos, our bodies appeared to be translucent as did the items around us. It was as if someone had partially erased us from the photos, allowing the wallpaper and art that should have been covered from view behind us to be seen *through* us. Images of spirit were everywhere as our own images shifted and moved about the room.

One of the most amazing photographs we captured contained spirit images of two Asian children laughing. One was so visible—it was easy to see his big loving smile as he radiated tremendous joy. The other child was younger and appeared to be shyer but it was obvious how loving and happy they were. The face of the healer appeared beside the spirit children in the photo, even though she was seated on the opposite side away from where they appeared. Unbeknownst to me, at the time of our scrying session, my friend was actively pursuing adopting two older children from another country. It was as if we were viewing a happy family photo from the future. That's when she confided that she was going through the adoption process and that what these children represented was a match to what she was looking for. Had her intentions manifested the children coming to her? Had the spirits of her future adopted children already selected her to be their parent through some sort of soul contract?

We also captured images of us from different times and places, as well as photos where we were both merged into one. It was as if both of our faces met in the middle and merged into one being with facial features on either side of the head.

Or as if someone had overlaid two images to create such an effect, except we viewed the photo immediately on the digital camera display screen and no adjustments were ever made.

Just for fun, we decided to see if we could influence the camera to take pictures a certain way. We both focused on a particular color, which we chose at random and agreed to. Then as we scryed, my husband photographed us and we focused on the color aqua blue. Much to our amazement, the next two pictures taken were all aqua blue! My husband freaked when he checked the display screen! It wasn't so much that he doubted us but that we had never ever tried to influence the outcome before. The entire frame was filled with aqua blue color and nothing else was detectable in the photo. Neither one of us showed up, nor did our table or candle. Even the dark-red Victorian wallpaper was invisible as everything was aqua blue. As soon as we stopped focusing on the aqua color, the photos returned to normal immediately.

The key to really getting good results is to believe in the process. Fear and doubt can sabotage the outcome. If you can, work with someone who has high energy. If at all possible, a medium or healer or someone really open minded will help produce the best results. Our scrying experiences have developed over time and really allowed us to grow in our own abilities. If you start with just the basics, your energy and abilities will grow too!

five

Transfiguration and Its History

Transfiguration is a term most often used by the Spiritualists to convey the ability to see spirits on the face of an advanced medium. This may occur in a séance setting but may also be demonstrated to a group of sitters. If you have used the information in this book to learn how to scry with success, then you are ready for the next step. It is a good idea to perfect your abilities to scry with others first so you become accustomed to raising your energy and holding it at a high vibration for an extended length of time. Transfiguration will require you to achieve and maintain a high vibration all on your own, without the aid of a scrying partner.

A medium who is proficient at transfiguration will be able to allow spirit faces to be seen by an entire audience of untrained sitters. However, there are many steps in between. As you begin your development of this technique, start with a small group of sitters before advancing to larger crowds.

Throughout history, there have been well-known mediums with the gift of physical mediumship that were able to demonstrate transfiguration to the public. It is an uncommon practice in the western world, and for many of you this may be the first time you experience it. Transfiguration occurs when a trance medium raises their vibration and allows spirit to draw ectoplasm from their body to show themselves in a mist-like substance in front of them. Ectoplasm is something all living beings have and it has been referred to as spiritual energy.

While researching the earliest mention of transfiguration, I found that the Bible mentions transfiguration in regard to Jesus. I include this information to demonstrate that the term has long been used throughout history. It seems that there exists a spiritual truth interwoven through all time. The New Testament (New International Version) has three parallel commentaries regarding the transfiguration of Jesus. Mark (9:2–12), Luke (9:28–36), and Matthew (17:1–3) all refer to this event in a similar manner.

Matthew (17:1–3). After six days Jesus took with Him Peter, James, and John, the brother of James, and led them up a high mountain by themselves. There He was transfigured before them. His face shone like the sun, and His clothes became as white as the light. Just then there appeared before them Moses and Elijah, talking with Jesus. (New International Version)

This may be one of the earliest historic accounts of a transfiguration.

I believe people have always had the ability to transfigure and connect with spirit, but it was not always safe to demonstrate these abilities in public. Perhaps that is why so little is written about the topic until the Spiritualist movement began.

Spiritualism is a religion that was established in the 1840s with the notoriety of the two Fox sisters, who lived in New York. They reported having spirit communication in the form of rappings on a table and claimed the ability to communicate with spirits. This early example of physical mediumship was demonstrated by asking questions and receiving knocks to indicate a specific answer.

This form of physical mediumship and two-way communication between the living and spirit world is often duplicated in modern paranormal research. From there, the religion spread across the ocean and was received in many parts of Europe. Spiritualism reached its peak between 1848 and the 1920s, and then waned due to fraudulent people working as mediums to capitalize on the tragedies of that era.

The Spiritualist National Union was established in the United Kingdom in 1901 to ensure the proper training and governing of practicing mediums. They also acted out against legislation that would prohibit mediums from being able to work publically. As many religions tried to prohibit spirit communication, the Spiritualists ensured that the valuable connection remained for us all. As spiritual beings, I believe we all have the ability to develop this gift. Though, it usually requires devoted practice to demonstrate it successfully.

Some famous transfiguration mediums from more recent times are Dianne Elliot and Queenie Nixon. Dianne Elliot (born 1938) had a natural ability to see spirits, but it is said that her work as a medium was influenced by transfigure medium Queenie Nixon (1918–1989). After attending a Spiritualist service where Queenie demonstrated transfiguration, Dianne was inspired to develop that same gift. She was formerly trained by UK medium Mavis Patella and spent many years in development. She attended Arthur Findlay College where she was tutored by Gordon Higginson (1918–1993) for physical mediumship.

Queenie Nixon also saw spirits as a youth and was encouraged to develop her mediumship gifts by the two aunties who raised her. She was also known for bringing forth direct voice, which denotes spirit voices speaking audibly in the séance room and not through the medium. Many people refer to audible spirit voices as disembodied voice. It is a clear, audible voice that seems to come from midair, without the presence of a spirit or living person.

The Spiritualist movement is largely responsible for bringing forth the research to help validate the spirit world and the ability to interact with it. Although the belief in spirits has been around since the beginning of mankind, it was Spiritualism that helped provide the proof that so many eager hearts longed for. For the first time, scientists began to study ectoplasm, the spirit's ability to affect electronics and the mysterious appearance of apports (physical items that appear or manifest directly from the spirit world).

Researching this phenomenon has helped to educate the public about psychic energy and the real gift of mediumship while at the same time exposing fraudulent practitioners (people who operate with gadgets or research their clients in an effort to trick them into believing they are having authentic spirit communications). I love verifiable proof and personally feel that Spiritualism was the catalyst for inciting the research necessary for validation. This field continues to grow as it inspires the invention of new electronic devices used to capture voices and manifestations of spirit for paranormal research worldwide.

American inventor Thomas Edison (1847–1931) was known worldwide for many of his inventions. The incandescent light bulb, phonograph, microphone, and movie camera are among his most well-known inventions. A lesser-known invention was one that Thomas Edison set out to create shortly before he died. He announced to the public that he was going to build a device to hear the voices of the dead. Yes, Edison believed that ghosts existed and also that they had a lot to say. It was his desire to invent a sort of spirit phone that would allow spirit voices to speak through to the living. Many people felt that if anyone could do it, Edison could.

Nikola Tesla (1856–1943) worked for Thomas Edison when he first immigrated to the United States. After a short time, he went off to work on his own, to experiment with a variety of electrical devices. Edison believed that Tesla was also building a device to speak to the dead. There was talk about Tesla receiving guidance for his work through some sort of spirits, and that they were communicating through radio frequencies that could not broadcast the human voice. This may have begun the race between Edison and Tesla to build the spirit phone and release it to the public.

Though it was written about, no device was ever brought forward to market. However, there have been claims after Edison's death that he did succeed in building such a device. Perhaps it didn't work as consistently as his other inventions so he thought he failed. But anyone working with spirit knows communication doesn't happen on demand. Today's devices are simple and effective, yet, there are times when they don't generate results and times that they do. It is perhaps best not to consider a device worthy of consistent results before first knowing that sometimes spirits cooperate and at other times they do not.

Needless to say, there have always been great minds in science and throughout history who have attempted to prove that life exists after death and capture results. There is not a lot of evidence gathered from transfiguration demonstrations, as the proof has always been in the eyes and hearts of the sitters. It is typically not advised to take photos during transfiguration because the white-light flash is thought to be harmful to the medium.

However, it is becoming possible to capture spirit essence during transfiguration in a similar way as photos can be taken during scrying sessions. Some modern-day mediums are experimenting with infrared or night vision cameras in completely dark rooms or perhaps even partial daylight demonstrations. This is still an exploratory field in terms of physical evidence.

Next, we will explore the various ways spirits let themselves be known during a séance and transfiguration.

Table Tipping Séance

Spirits can interact during a séance in a multitude of ways. The most common form of communication would be spoken through the voice of the attending medium. However, spirit orbs can manifest, direct or disembodied voices from spirit may be heard, physical sensations and touch can be felt, and there can be apports and movement of physical items around the séance room. This would often include bells and trumpets, which are common séance room tools. Though it is not limited to those items, as lights, bangs, and knocks can also occur, as well as any item being moved from one place to the next. Transfiguration may occur during a séance as well, though it is more common for it to occur during a demonstration for that purpose.

There has been some debate over the spirit orb or balls of light that appear during a séance, which are more commonly photographed now by ordinary people. While some indicate the color of the orb has differential meanings, others look for spirit faces that appear within the ball of light to identify the spirit present. I have had ample experience photographing spirit orbs and have come to believe that they may represent any spiritual being. It may be the spirit presence of a loved one, a ghost, angel, or nature spirit. Orbs seem to be the vehicle in which spiritual beings travel. It is best to keep an open mind when witnessing a spirit orb and trying to determine who or what it is.

Cassadaga is a Spiritualist Camp in Florida where every resident is a licensed and trained medium. They offer mediumship service, private sittings, and a variety of different séance experiences. In 2008, I had the opportunity to go there with my husband and daughter. Not knowing that most people booked sessions in advance, we breezed into town and attended the first public demonstration available. This was my first experience to witness a group mediumship demonstration. Afterward, we visited the bookstore and browsed through a rather large assortment of business cards for local mediums.

The energy in the town was electric and I was excited to be there. We gathered a stack of business cards and began to call to arrange a professional séance. Much to our dismay, the mediums were already booked solid. We explained our situation and that we were only in town overnight. Thankfully, the medium who we really wanted to work with was willing to overbook to accommodate us.

Victor Vogenitz and his wife Esther showed up to unlock the séance room at the chapel. We were in for a treat because his specialty was old-fashioned table tipping. I had heard about it but had never experienced it before and, quite frankly, had my doubts. Table tipping was a common Victorian-era type of séance that began in the mid to late 1800s. Victor was not put off by my doubts, as he had been investigated by many people before us and was found to be authentic. Many investigations were actually well publicized in his favor. We sat back and decided to just have fun and see what happened.

Victor and Esther were very good about explaining everything to us as first-time sitters. We were encouraged to inspect the trumpets, which are often called "spirit trumpets." They are one to three feet tall cone-shaped items that can collapse into themselves. Trumpets are said to help magnify spirit voices, making them easier to hear. However, we learned that they may also be moved by spirit, either through collapsing, tipping over, or vibrating on the table. We looked under the table and inspected the room for hidden cords or strings too. Although we didn't really know what we were looking for, it was easy to determine that there were no strings attached to the table or anything else.

Victor showed us how heavy the table was at the beginning of the séance and said that we could compare it to how light it would be afterward. As the séance got underway, the lights were turned out and the room was completely dark. We could only see the illumination of the trumpets because glow-in-the-dark tape was adhered to them. They sat on top of the table where our hands were resting.

We were guided to sing songs as a way to raise the vibration in the room. As we sang, we began to move the table by spinning it clockwise and moving one hand over the other as we pulled the heavy table along. It took quite an effort for all of us to move it at first but as the séance continued, the table moved with greater ease. Through this process, the table began to respond to us as if it was being influenced by spirit presence. When there was a spirit message for my daughter, the table would stop spinning and tip toward her. Victor was able to connect with the spirit of her loved one and bring forward a message of healing. After which, we would resume spinning the table and singing again.

The séance continued in this fashion, table stopping, tipping, and sometimes moving itself from side to side while Victor gave messages. It was a fun and heartwarming experience, having felt a real connection to the spirits that Victor brought through. When the séance was done, the lights were turned back on and we stayed to chat while they put their spirit tools away for the night. Victor told us to move the table again and compare it to the way it felt just prior to our séance. I put my hand on the table to see if I could spin it alone and it felt like an entirely different table! It had become so light that it now moved freely.

Victor explained that while we are working with spirit in a high vibration, the particles of the table seem to get temporarily displaced. The table is always lighter and easier to move after a séance and can literally levitate if it is used in continual séances. They had also had that phenomenon studied and verified, which spoke to the practical side of me. I felt the table before the séance and again afterward. No one had to tell me that the energy had altered the weight of the table; I concluded that for myself.

Afterward, we all went out to the pond behind the chapel where we were guided to take spirit photos. Upon death, many of the Spiritualists had chosen to be cremated and have their ashes sprinkled in that pond. It was a well-known hot spot for spirit activity. Sure enough, we captured many orb photos and even had interactive experiences with them. We asked one to land on our hands and then photographed a perfect orb resting on our open palms.

Visiting Cassadaga reignited the enthusiasm I had felt all my life about the spirit world. It reminded me of being thirteen years old and having sleepover parties where we attempted to communicate with spirits through the Ouija Board or lift each other after chanting "light as a feather." At last, my adult self could experience these events with a mature perspective and I felt compelled to learn and experience more.

Cabinet Séance

Cabinet séances were first made popular in the 1850s by the Davenport brothers. They are used by physical mediums to demonstrate transfiguration. The cabinet was built of wood and was meant to confine the medium as a means to authenticate the process. The mediums were often situated on a chair inside the cabinet with hands and feet bound. The cabinet continued to become a favorite tool for physical mediums as it was believed to contain the buildup of spirit energy, making manifestations of spirit easier. In modern day, the same phenomenon may be experienced in the common shower stall with curtain drawn as this is known to build spirit energy in the same manner.

In 2010, I flew to England to attend classes at Arthur Findlay College, known as the world's foremost college for the advancement of spiritualism and psychic sciences. The school employed the finest mediums and teachers from around the world. The classes were scheduled from 9:00 a.m. to 5:00 p.m. with events and demonstrations being offered each evening. Toward the end of the course, the students were all invited to attend a cabinet séance by one of Arthur Findlay's finest physical mediums.

The room was filled with approximately 100 students, eager to see spirit manifest. I had no previous experience with cabinet séances, so this was a first for me. The cabinet looked like an old-fashioned telephone booth with a chair inside for the medium to sit on. There was a red light attached to the top of the cabinet that shined directly down on the medium's face. Once inside, the medium went into meditation or trance and began to build energy. There were multiple trained mediums outside the cabinet who went into meditation to help raise the vibration in the room to assist with the process.

As the energy began to build, we could all see small balls of light flying through the air as wefts of ectoplasm left the medium's face. The ectoplasm resembled a large puff of smoke that appeared as quickly as it disappeared. We also heard the sound of bells ringing that seemed to be coming from midair above our heads. Bells are a common séance tool, thought to be rung by the presence of spirit, with or without the actual bell being moved. In this case, we had a perfect line of sight, and the bells sat motionless upon the stage. Only the sound of them ringing was heard by the students.

Silence overtook the room again as the students stared in anticipation. Suddenly, we began to see spirit faces emerge upon the medium's face inside the cabinet. The succession of faces began to happen very quickly and I nudged the student sitting beside me to share the excitement. She remarked that she was not seeing anything happen yet. Some of the other students sitting beside me did not see the spirit faces, though many students did. I surmised that the scrying technique had prepared me to see spirit and had helped to develop my clairvoyant abilities.

In the next section, you will learn how to properly prepare for transfiguration, to ensure that your séances are safe, fun, and bring healing to those in attendance.

How to Transfigure

Before you begin, it is of the utmost importance that you are comfortable with the concept of holding a séance. The word séance simply means to sit for spirit. Some of you already feel totally comfortable with this term, but others may still feel a tinge of fear associated with that word. For some, the belief that séances are negative is held on the genetic and group consciousness level. That simply means that your ancestors may have experienced fear surrounding the topic of séances and you inherited the fear in your cells. If you absorbed the fear from group consciousness instead, just release it gently. Know that much of the fear was impressed upon mediums through religious dogma or belief systems that did not encourage people to connect with spirit on their own. It is perfectly fine to call it something else so that you are not triggered in any way. For that reason, we will refer to séance as sitting or sitting for spirit.

Here is what you will need before you get started:

- A large black cloth to use as a backdrop on the wall—purchase several yards of a thick, black fabric to be used for this purpose.
- A red light—a typical party light will not work. Red light bulbs in 7.5-10 watts may be ordered online.
- An extension cord with dimmer—most hardware stores will have this.

- Black shirt and pants—turtleneck or long sleeve will work great.
- Chairs for medium and sitters.
- Completely dark room—basement or garage works best or cover all windows.
- Lamp—clamp-on lamps with a long, narrow shade work best. You may tape on an extra piece of cardboard or thick paper to elongate the shade, making it easier to aim at a narrow location. Paper bags work pretty well for this. If you tape on an extension, it should be about 1½ to 2 feet in length, creating a sort of spotlight.

Roles

Everyone has a job. The medium will be sitting in the chair facing the audience of sitters.

One person will control the lights to ensure no white light is turned on during the sitting. No cell phones or cameras are allowed. When the medium is ready to begin, he or she will meditate to raise their energy. Say a prayer of protection or set your intention of allowing only the spirits of loved ones or highest and best to come through:

"Creator, I ask to be of service to the sitters gathered here in the highest and best way. Allow me to connect with and bring forward spirit of loved ones for the purpose of healing. Thank you."

The light monitor will turn off any overhead or room lights while turning on the red light. Make sure that the red light illuminates only the face of the medium and not the surrounding area. The person in charge of the lights will be able to dim the red light accordingly to reach the correct level of visibility. This is achieved through trial and error. Start on a very dim setting where the face of the medium is just barely showing and then raise and lower the dimmer based on the outcome. Once the session gets underway, leave the light in the same position so that there are no false results coming from the variations of light.

The audience will contribute their energy to having a successful outcome. This is where transfiguration mostly differs from the scrying technique. Holding a quiet concentration while scrying helps to raise the energy in the room and "drop" the veil. During transfiguration the focus will be on the medium, who will need ample energy to produce physical mediumship results. In this case, singing, laughing, and talking are found most helpful to raise the vibration in the room.

When the room feels charged with energy, the sitters can call out to the spirits with whom they wish to contact. It is okay to be playful and spontaneous while this is going on as the spirit world welcomes joy and excitement. Everyone present should remain seated for the duration of the event.

Speak to the spirits and thank them for coming. You may say things like, "Welcome spirits. Thank you for joining us. Is my grandma (call her by name) here with us? Can you please come and visit me so that I can see your face again? Who is here with us? Thank you for showing up. Do you still like to cook? Have you seen your grandchild? We are all doing well here and wanted to say hello." Keep the energy raised through continual speaking. If the energy drops, the spirit faces presenting themselves will slow down or stop entirely.

The audience should begin singing to raise the vibration in the room again. Singing fun, uplifting songs works best. One of my favorites is, *She'll be coming around the mountain when she comes* ... make sure to throw in a "*yee ha!*" You could also sing holiday songs that are upbeat such as "Rudolph the Red Nosed Reindeer," "Frosty the Snowman," or any song that suits you.

The sitting may take approximately thirty minutes to an hour. If it goes any longer, the energy will wane and the spirits most likely will not be able to manifest. As long as there is energy in the room and the spirits are presenting themselves, it is fine to continue.

When you feel the session is coming to a close, everyone should give thanks to the spirits for coming through and allowing everyone to witness them and reconnect. The medium should bring all their energy back into themselves and make an energy break mentally or physically (however you prefer). One way to do this is by slicing your hand through the air from the bottom of your root chakra (tailbone area) to the top of your crown chakra (above your head). It's a good idea for the audience to also make an energy break by imagining that the area around them is bathed in white light and cleared of any residual energy from spirit. It may also be a good idea for everyone present to engage in prayer, giving gratitude and commanding a clearing of the space:

"We thank all the spirits for coming and allowing us to reconnect with you. We ask at this time that all energy is restored in our highest and best way. Clear any residual energy from us and our space now. Thank you."

The light monitor may turn the red light up to its brightest position and when the medium gives a clear indication that he or she is ready, the other lights in the room may be turned on.

As you progress in your development, it may be acceptable to use infrared or night vision cameras to capture the spirit faces. Always ask for the permission of the spirits beforehand. Sometimes, when this is attempted without seeking permission, spirit avoids the session entirely. Be sure to check in with your own spirit team and make sure that you have permission for photography. The permissions may be granted to the medium (not the sitters) and will depend upon the medium's skill level.

While transfiguring, ectoplasm is released and the flash of a camera could cause it to snap back into the medium too quickly. This is believed to be dangerous to the medium and could cause physical harm. Under no conditions should anyone take photos or turn on the lights until the transfiguration session is complete and the light monitor declares it okay. There have only been a few mediums to date who have been able to transfigure in daylight and also capture photographic evidence.

Remember, this is a process. Start at the beginning and allow yourself to advance in a comfortable way. Your spirit team will work with your body's chemistry to allow the changes to occur at your own rate.

There exists a phenomenon that once one person breaks an existing limit or sets a new standard, others will be able to advance much easier. This happens in sports and other record-breaking feats and is true for mediumship and transfiguration as well. The dedication of one person may benefit all who follow. Always give recognition and thanks to the mediums who proceeded you.

Preparing for Transfiguration

The sitters will have little to do but witness and sing, so we will introduce some strategies to prepare the medium. When doing any type of psychic or mediumship work, it helps to keep your body light by eating extra healthy the day of the sitting. Dairy (cow's milk, cheese, butter) should be avoided. It is best to also avoid heavy meals containing red meat. It is beneficial to eat a lot of greens, salads, or any kind of super foods mixed into a smoothie. Nutrition is a key component of increasing spiritual energy. When the medium is done, they may actually crave some grounding food and this can be accomplished by eating the meat and dairy that they avoided earlier in the day.

The medium should have a good grasp on meditation to be sure they know how to clear their mind and focus their energy. Successful transfiguration mediums will not impose themselves into the demonstration, but rather, take a back seat and hold the energy for spirit. You may use any meditation that you wish to in an effort to release any troubles from the day. Clear your mind of any concerns and especially any fears of failure while demonstrating. The medium's role is actually quite passive while transfiguration is going on. If they have prepared their body by eating light, healthy meals and prepared their mind by clearing it, it will be easy for spirit to work with their energy and manifest for the audience.

If you already practice a healing modality or have a particular ritual used for raising your energy, feel free to use it. As we discovered while scrying, this can amplify the energy and help to produce incredible results. Use what you know and apply it to your transfiguration. If you are new to meditation and working with energy, you may find the meditation here useful.

Meditation to Prepare

Sit straight up with your back and shoulders erect, feet flat on the floor and hands facing upward while resting on your knees. Relax and take a deep breath in, filling your lungs and then slowly blowing it out through pursed lips. Repeat this three times. (Breath work is a very important part of meditation and relaxation, so don't skip this part!) Expand your energy into the chair you are sitting on, and imagine that you fill the room around you. Become one with everything, every particle, every object. Feel connected to everything as you allow yourself to expand even further into the town that you live in, then out into the state, the country, the planet. Feel yourself as you connect to all the energy in the universe.

Imagine that all your troubles and worries are being gently lifted out of you, leaving your body and being transformed back into balance in the universe. Allow this energy to leave and as it does, it removes any blocks that you have for doing this work. Release all your fears and doubts, also witnessing it as it reaches the heavens, transforming into light and perfect balance.

Know that you are one with everything in creation. Call upon your angels, guides, and spirit team to come in and assist you. Allow yourself to be filled with unconditional love and peace and actually witness this as light comes into your body to fill you up. This process naturally raises your energy and allows you to gain a higher connection.

If you find yourself thinking about your day or any worries, take more deep breaths in and blow it out through pursed lips. Repeat at least three times to help you release … and relax …

Now, ask that your loved ones in spirit, your angels, and your spirit team assist you with your demonstration, keeping you safe, protected, and fully capable of producing results for your sitters. Call in the loved ones of your sitters and invite them to work through your energy to help bring closure, love, and comfort to their surviving family. Always ask that you may be of service to spirit in the highest and best way.

As you sit for demonstration, keep your eyes closed. You may speak, as you will be calling in spirits and communicating with your sitters. Welcome everyone and invite them to begin calling in their loved ones. You may feel energy coming up your spine that makes you want to move slightly; this is spirit preparing you for channeling. If you feel guided to speak aloud to your sitters, know that this may be how spirit has chosen to use your energy. Relax and enjoy the experience.

Always remember that this is not a parlor trick. Transfiguration allows the medium to be of service to spirit and the living by bringing forward proof of life and to help foster healing for all parties. While this is fun and exciting, the main goal is to provide healing. If you remember this, you will be able to stay out of your own way and allow the spirits to manifest through your energy.

The more you meditate, the more you will become aware of all the amazing spirits that assist you. If you haven't already taken the time to get to know your spirit guide team, now would be a good time to do that. Your spirit guide team is assigned to help you through your life. When you decide to develop your skills as a medium, you may notice that you have a change in guides. Some guides, especially deceased family members who have chosen to be your guides, will stay with you. However, the other helpers in the spirit world come and go depending on what you are doing and what kind of help you need.

If you decided to develop your skills as an artist, you would attract in a new set of guides to inspire your creativity. They would have been people who lived physical lifetimes as artists or they may be angelic. Even the nature spirits can inspire artists as they love the energy of joy and creating. The same goes for mediumship. Perhaps you have already begun to learn mediumship and have noticed the energy around you changing. Oftentimes, a developing medium will feel a slight buzzing sensation around their body. This is typical of how your spirit team works with and adjusts your energy to prepare you for mediumship work. You will develop a sensitivity to the spirit world around you as you attract more spirit helpers to your team. Their goal is to help you, but it is best for you to ask for their help and be specific about what you want. Thank them for coming in to work with you, acknowledge their presence, and ask them to introduce themselves to you. Developing your relationship with your guides will be very helpful in any spiritual work that you pursue.

It is my preference to call upon my highest guides for any given situation. I like to clear them through the Creator to make sure they are who they say they are and that their energy is pure.

To clear your guides with Creator, go into prayer or meditation, send your energy high above your physical space, and imagine you are connected to Creator. The energy of creation is where people go to seek God or Creator; it is a higher plane than the guides, or even the ascended masters are on. However, whatever higher power you feel comfortable with is what you should use.

Once you feel a clear connection to divine energy, present each guide and request to know if they are in your highest and best to work with. If you have inadvertently attracted one that isn't, they most likely won't even appear before Creator or at this vibrational frequency. This is a good indication that they were not in your highest and best to work with and may have attempted to lead you astray.

It is best to let those ones go as they can really wreak havoc on your ego and work. Once you have cleared each guide with Creator, you may feel confident to proceed with them and allow their guidance to lead you.

Transfiguration Demonstration

Transfiguration further enhanced my understanding of the spirit world and I was most influenced by the work of Spiritualist medium, Reverend John Lilek. Rev. John dedicated his life to developing his gifts as a transfiguration medium and was the best I have ever seen.

Most mediumship is referred to as mental mediumship because the images and messages are primarily delivered through the thoughts of the medium. Transfiguration mediumship is a form of physical mediumship where a medium is able to amplify his energy to produce physical phenomenon to take place. During a transfiguration, many spirit faces appear in a sort of mist just in front of the medium's face. As noted before, that energy is often referred to as ectoplasm.

I had begun to spontaneously experience a version of this phenomenon during healing sessions with clients. During one normal healing session, I opened my eyes and saw the clear, transfigured image of my client's deceased mother superimposed over her face. When that happens, it is more of a gift from the spirit world as they have decided to step in for a particular reason. The spirit is able to use the energy of both the medium and sitter as well as the energy produced during a healing session. While it is not the focus of a healing session, it does happen. However, a transfiguration medium has the ability to call in spirits and have them appear physically over their own face for the sitter or audience to see. They may call upon loved ones and even historical figures that many people are familiar with.

There are few mediums who can demonstrate physical mediumship and fewer still that can produce transfiguration. After years of humble and dedicated practice, Rev. John was able to demonstrate transfiguration mediumship to large audiences with ease. His demonstrations often included other physical phenomenon such as physical touch, floating lights, spirit voices, and multiple images of full-bodied spirit apparitions. He had the ability to amplify his energy and call in spirit that could be seen and experienced by an entire audience of untrained sitters.

In 2013, I was introduced to Rev. John Lilek through a close personal friend who had attended his transfiguration demonstration. I was thrilled to connect with a transfiguration medium in the United States. I discussed my previous sitting for the cabinet séance and questioned why not all of the students could witness the transfiguration. Rev. John explained it to me in terms of energy. Starting out, a medium may be able to raise their energy high enough for a few sitters to witness spirit, while a medium with the ability to raise their energy higher could demonstrate for an entire crowd with success. He told me that he had been very devoted to his development and had acquired the ability to raise his energy to that level.

After a brief conversation by phone, I invited him to demonstrate in our home. Rev. John and his wife Greta were demonstrating all over the United States and worked their way to Wisconsin for a spirit-filled weekend.

My husband and I helped Rev. John set up the room for transfiguration. He explained how important it was to keep the room dimly lit with the use of one red light and no white light. He reiterated that turning on a white light at any time during the transfiguration could be harmful to the medium as the ectoplasm could snap back into the physical body too fast. His trusted wife Greta was in charge of the light switch to ensure that no one turned it on prematurely.

The setup was actually quite simple. We decided to hold the event in the basement of our large Victorian home because it was the only space that we could provide darkness without the glare of streetlights or car lights passing by. We hung a red light from the ceiling and aimed it at the chair that Rev. John was due to sit in for the demonstration. The light had a dimmer so we could adjust the lighting just right to capture the movement of spirit faces. We hung a large, black sheet of fabric along the entire wall behind his chair and the rest of the room was filled with folding chairs facing forward. The setup was so simple that I thought it lended more credibility to the demonstration. Just as we finished, people began to arrive.

The night of his sold-out event, everyone squeezed into our dark basement filled with folding chairs. Many of the people present for the sitting were seasoned healers and mediums but none had seen a transfiguration before. Perhaps they were there out of curiosity more than anything, or the desire to see spirit with their own eyes. We greeted everyone and led them to the basement chairs to await the demonstration. Rev. John walked around outside, avoiding the crowd as he gathered his energy and connected to spirit. He was the last to enter the room and took his seat in front of the crowd. Rev. John was wearing all black, which allowed him to blend into the background. As my husband, daughter, and I sat in the back row, Greta dimmed the lights and focused the red light directly upon his face. The transfiguration was underway.

The audience was guided to raise the energy in the room by reciting, "welcome spirits," and calling for their deceased loved ones by name. We were pre-warned that if we gasped in awe and stared silently at the spirit faces, the energy would fade. Instead, we were told to assist the process by keeping the energy in the room high and were guided to speak encouraging words to spirit. However, when the spirit faces began to emerge on Rev. John's face, we forgot our duty and stared in complete awe anyway.

A moment or two passed as a few people remembered to speak. "Thank you spirits," "we see you." Others joined in as the audience began to interact, allowing the spirits to manifest one after the next. Unlike my previous experience with the cabinet séance, I noticed that everyone present was actively witnessing the spirit faces. Abraham Lincoln, George Washington, and many other recognizable faces from history were clearly seen in succession. The audience began to call for specific loved ones in spirit, and the familiar faces of family began to show themselves too. The fact that everyone in the room could see the same faces and identify them simultaneously dispelled any thoughts that we were just seeing what we wanted to see.

As the transfiguration continued, the crowd expressed sincere and utter shock as they were indeed seeing spirit for themselves. Many sitters witnessed the spirits of close family members and friends whom they had deep personal connections with. I tried to debunk the possibility that spirits of loved ones were able to pop in with such ease but could not. Rev. John had no idea what our family members and friends in spirit looked like. He had only met the sitters on their way into the basement moments earlier.

When he brought through a famous or historical figure, everyone could easily recognize them. I wondered if there was some sort of collective consciousness or mass hallucination going on. But when Rev. John brought through a common person, a relative that only one person could recognize, I had to rethink how this worked.

He also brought through spirit that several of the sitters knew in life, and each time, all those reacted with the same recognition of the spirit presenting itself. My skepticism faded as the demonstration continued on. There was no possible way to produce a specific face that only one sitter would recognize. I came to the conclusion that this phenomenon was real and allowed the experience to unfold in front of me.

I personally witnessed many loved ones in spirit as they appeared in this manner. My husband and daughter recognized several close family members at the same exact moments that I did. We called out for a family friend and each time, he appeared right away. Though several attempts were only partial manifestations that showed half of his face, we still recognized his features. Other times, he would emerge in perfect full form.

Some of the guests also received messages from spirit as Rev. John allowed his voice to be used by channeled spirit. When this happened, the image would appear and scan the crowd for their living loved one, then relay a message. The voices were often in an accent or a variety of tonal ranges as the messages were confirmed valid by the sitters. The image would sustain itself until the message was complete and then the parade of spirit faces would resume.

We continued to call upon our loved ones by name to keep the energy high and to let the spirits know that they were welcome. I paid close attention to the entourage of spirits but failed to see one particular family member that

I wanted to connect with. I patiently watched and called her name.

Rev. John told us if we saw his eyes open that we were actually seeing spirit eyes, because his physical eyes remained closed throughout the demonstration. This actually happened a few times as we all witnessed spirit eyes glancing upon the crowd. The images appearing in the ectoplasm seemed to grow and shrink depending on who was coming through. When Abraham Lincoln came through, the ectoplasm grew very high to accommodate his tall stature and top hat. Through the mist, we could still see Rev. John, sitting with his eyes closed, and quite a bit shorter than the spirit image.

We witnessed many spirit faces with different facial features, hairstyles, and personal accessories. Some of the audience members called out to their spirit guides and they quickly showed themselves too. At this point, we began to see a wider variety of images, including many Native Americans and indigenous people belonging to different tribes or cultures from around the world. A few times, I witnessed a complete image of a head, neck, and upper torso emerge out of the middle of Rev. John's body and turn to look at me with eyes open. I did not recognize this image; however, we were told that many spirit guides would try to make contact with us during the demonstration. When this happened, no one saw the spirit but me. It is difficult to describe what a strange occurrence this is, because I saw the spirit with such clarity.

We also saw some freaky, non-human images. They were interesting to see because we had to confront our own fears and judgments regarding entities that didn't look like us.

Several of us were spooked when we saw an image that appeared to be non-human, with glowing eyes and an ugly face. We assumed it was a menacing spirit but then remembered we had said prayers for protection before we began and realized that we were safe. By saying our prayer for protection and maintaining a high vibration in the room, we were assured that the spirits coming through would also be of a high vibration. Although, this is a good place to remind you that you should clear your energy and the room after every sitting, no matter what.

Some people in the audience received a healing from the spirits that they described as a hot, tingly sensation in the area of the body that needed healing. I called out for my little sister one more time because she was the only loved one I didn't see transfigured. Other loved ones continued to come through for the crowd while I waited and watched.

As I stilled myself in silent anticipation, I became aware of a presence standing slightly behind me to my right and then felt several taps on my shoulder. I knew immediately that this was my sister tapping me to let me know she was there with me. She didn't need to show up in the ectoplasm because she was standing beside me the whole time. It's worth mentioning here, that as a host, I made sure to sit in the back of the room. There was no one behind me and my chair was backed up to the brick wall. I had been touched by spirit before and knew that the simple touch of a spirit finger could instantly transfer the identity and communicate a message of love. I was so pleased to know my sister was there with me.

The transfiguration was the most physical display of spirit manifestation that I had ever encountered. While early séances would have paled in comparison, perhaps the energies are more conducive for physical mediumship now. Original séance rooms were notably dark with no means of light whatsoever. This may have made it too easy for fraudulent mediums to attempt parlor tricks to fool naïve crowds. Undoubtedly, this part of history has left a bad taste in the collective mouth of society. I found myself examining and re-examining every aspect of the séance room and demonstration for authenticity. Perhaps we all suffer a little lost faith, which causes us to be more skeptical of mediums in general.

Some television shows and mainstream media often regard séances as hokey, Victorian-era entertainment and not something a rational, grounded individual would attend. Or worse yet, religions proclaim they are dangerous or evil. However, people have been communicating with the dead since the beginning of time.

Perhaps people know more about the spirit world now than ever before and are able to dispel all the superstition surrounding it. This is possibly due to the popularity of paranormal groups, ghost hunting shows, and electronic devices simple enough to use that even a novice can record a spirit voice. (Perhaps we should thank Edison and Tesla for the early attempts at the spirit phone!)

We now know that the spirit world consists of a variety of energies, ranging from low to high and that the frequency of spirit is just slightly higher than our own. We have learned that it is possible to raise our own frequency, making it easier to access the spirit world. Perhaps the vibrational shift on the planet has brought about more awareness and increased abilities. Today's mediums are capable of much more than earlier mediums, given the same dedication.

I consider myself a believer as much as I am a skeptic, but sometimes seeing is believing. Witnessing the transfiguration séance was a truly unique experience for me because it provided clear visual proof of spirit and authenticated transfiguration. Even though I am a medium and spirits have been contacting me my whole life, I still like to discern information through personal experience while I continue to collect evidence.

Transfer of Transfiguration

On the last day of Rev. John's visit, he offered to give me a gift that he called a spirit transfusion. He said I already had the ability to transfigure, though I may have been unaware of it. A spirit transfusion is when a very developed physical medium sends energy to a lesser-developed medium so they may both transfigure together. I sat beside Rev. John in front of five sitters in the darkened room with red light illuminating both our faces. Two of our guests were completely new to this phenomenon and just came with open hearts and minds. My husband and daughter were present, along with Greta, who was managing the lights.

As soon as the lights dimmed, the small crowd of sitters began to see spirit faces emerge on both of our faces. My husband described what he saw as a white, misty energy come out from the side of Rev. John's head, stretching the appearance of his ear toward my head. He saw a bow tie effect as the energy from Rev. John and my own energy blended together. My husband said it quite literally looked like a transfusion of energy.

I felt very calm with a slight tingly sensation over my face, as if cobwebs were dangling over me. I didn't enter a trance of any kind; I just relaxed and closed my eyes. As Rev. John called out to many spirits, I silently called to some of my own. I called some Archangels, Mother Mary, and then some family members who had passed.

The sitters commented that they saw a woman wearing a habit (as seen with religious orders) and then they exclaimed that it was Mother Mary. Immediately after, my nose broadened, and my hairstyle changed as my husband and daughter both recognized my little sister simultaneously. They also saw an image appear with a very elongated face beginning wide at the forehead and narrowing greatly at the chin. The spirit eyes opened and looked directly at them. Though the eyes appeared to be black, they were described as being beautiful and filled with compassion and love. They felt it was a female extraterrestrial, but not like any they had seen on television.

Our friends were pretty shocked to see the many spirit faces and began to call upon their loved ones too. After seeing several recognizable faces, one sitter called out for her grandma. She was very close to her grandma and had really hoped to make contact with her at the séance. She called out again but didn't see her. Then, just as it had happened to me the night before, she got touched on her shoulder. She knew immediately that this touch was from the hand of her grandma in spirit and that she had received a healing.

Calling to the spirits of your loved ones allows them to connect into your energy so that they may be seen and felt at this vibrational plane. This experience really solidified my belief that our loved ones do hear our thoughts as much as our words. When Rev. John called to spirit, they showed up. When I silently thought about spirit, they showed up as well. Even the ascended masters appeared when called upon.

An ascended master is a being of light (spirit) who is no longer in a body and who transcended physical form through awakening and raising consciousness to a pure state while still living. They no longer need to work out karma or participate in the life and death and rebirth cycle. An ascended master is one who has "mastered" their physical and spiritual selves and who serves others from the spirit realm. Jesus, Mother Mary, Buddha, St. Germain, Kuthumi, Melchizedek, Confucius, Kwan Yin, and dozens of others are regarded as ascended masters.

Approximately a year after this event, Rev. John passed away. He was truly a gifted medium and, in my opinion, the best transfiguration medium in modern times. I feel privileged to have witnessed his demonstration as well as to have had the opportunity to sit beside him to demonstrate. He was so willing to share his gift with others, and even on his deathbed claimed that he would be available to assist anyone who had a sincere desire to be of service to spirit. So, though you may not have known him personally, feel free to call upon him for help as you develop. He is a regular at our demonstrations and stops by frequently to encourage us to share the work.

Notes From Greta

Noted transfiguration medium, Reverend John Lilek passed into the spirit world in August 2014. His devoted wife Greta worked beside John as they toured the United States, demonstrating mediumship and transfiguration for large crowds. Below are some of the firsthand experiences shared by Greta.

> "We will always be students of today and teachers of tomorrow, as well as Teachers of today and Students of tomorrow. Good Tools make good works when we call upon the inspiration of God, our works then become like that of a chisel a cut above the rest."
> —Reverend John Lilek

Cassadaga 2012

John and Greta visited the Cassadage Spiritual Camp in Central Florida in 2012. Greta described the experience:

> We were setting up to do a séance for the public and the room was nearly full. A bus pulled up with an unexpected group of about ten more people. They came to see John demonstrate transfiguration after one of the party had been to a demonstration earlier in the week and had witnessed the phenomena. After asking his spirit guides for permission, John allowed them to join us. The room was so full now that the back row was standing.
>
> The séance got under way. We sang songs and the vibration in the room was really high. Our regular batteries (skilled mediums who meditate to increase

energy in the room to help the demonstration) were Jodie Martinez, Michael Taylor, and Sven and Gail, who all lived in the camp. We all sat in the front row encouraging people to keep the vibration raised.

We witnessed Abraham Lincoln, Richard Nixon, and many loved ones. People were recognizing their loved ones and they received many messages through John, who was in light trance drifting in and out as each spirit came and left.

All of a sudden a young Hispanic man in the group of ten called out a name and got very excited, talking to a woman who sat next to him. The woman recognized one of her twins, who had passed to spirit, then she saw the second twin over John's face; several others of the party saw them also. She received the most loving messages and was reassured that the twins were well and happy and watching over her. John gave several confirming messages to her and she began to cry quietly. The room was in complete silence during these messages.

Afterward several of the group told John that the woman had been confined to her house because of her grief and was talked into coming to the séance at the last minute by the friend who had previously been to the transfiguration. She had lost the twins in a terrible accident several years before.

The next year, while demonstating in Cassadaga again, one of the same party came to John for a reading and told him that the lady now had peace and was leading a grief-free life and thanked John for for the gift of seeing and talking to her children again.

Séance in Indiana

This was a duel sitting with Rev. Christine Sabick and Rev. John Lilek. Greta described the experience:

We opened up the séance and straight away had lots of blue orbs around John's head; the trumpets were slightly moving, appearing to grow tall then back to normal size. I sat next to Rev. Andie Hollis when I noticed a blue light just above her head slightly to the right. I watched for several minutes and it moved in front of her, she saw it and so did her husband Rev. Michael Sabick. We watched it dance all around her head for fifteen to twenty minutes.

John in trance gave a name and Andie confirmed it was the daughter of her friend. As the name was given it responded by moving to the back of her head then returned to the front.

After the séance Andie told the circle that her friend's daughter had passed away that morning after a long battle with cancer.

Love and Lights

Greta said this séance was the most emotional for her:

John was very sick with terminal lung cancer. Several friends had traveled to Maine from California and Florida to say their goodbyes to John. John insisted that he do a séance in our séance room at home. This was against my wishes but he was adamant that he sat.

Present was Rev. Rachael Slifco, a dear friend from California; Jodie Martinez and her daughter from Cassadaga, Florida; Theresa and Cory from Maine; and several of our regular sitters. The room filled with wonderful colored lights and even before John had finished his opening prayers the lights were red, yellow, blue, and white.

The trumpet on John's left seemed to morph. Everyone witnessed it moving up and down and then it faded and disappeared. John gave a very emotional message to me and everyone in the room. Spirit said they were overjoyed that he was soon to be united with them.

Rev. James Tingley, John's mentor, appeared over John's face. Several people confirmed that it was him from photos in the séance room shown after the séance. Mabel Riffel came through to say she was looking forward to being with John and working with him. Mabel was a famous Camp Chesterfield medium who often came through John's séances. John has her chair and trumpet in our séance room bequeathed to him from Rev. Tingley.

The room filled with the most beautiful lights and the energy was filled with love. At the end of the séance, as John was closing with prayer and thanks, the trumpet that had disappeared re-appeared in front of the curtain that John sat behind. When the lights went on, Theresa touched it and it felt hot.

Five days after this séance John said goodbye to the physical world and joined his beloved mentor Rev. James Tingley. John was looking forward during these last days to meeting Jim again; he told me he was sad that he was leaving me after such a short time, but reassured me he would help me and would come to collect me when my time comes to go home to Spirit.

He has kept his word, constantly giving confirmational messages through mediums we have had the privilege to work with during our time together. He regularly visits all his students and they keep me informed of the work they are doing with John.

In Rev. John Lilek's career as a transfiguration medium, he was able to produce extraordinary results. People who sat for John's demonstrations claimed to see spirits manifest and walk around the room, experiences of physical touch, see colored lights, spirit hands, and multiple full-bodied spirit apparitions appear on or near him.

Our Transfiguration Experiences
Christmas Spirit

It was Christmastime and our adult children and their partners were visiting for a few days when we decided to do a transfiguration for them. My husband decided to sit for the kids while I had the responsibility of keeping the energy high and controlling the lights. We established our sitting room in a lower-level bathroom because it was dark and easy to access. We hung our black cloth along the back wall to completely cover the vanity mirror and light fixture. The double sink counter worked as a bench seat for the medium and that was covered in black cloth as well. We brought in a few folding chairs, set up our red light on the dimmer, and took turns being the light controller.

My husband sat upon the counter and was wearing all black. We covered his lower half with a black cloth so that we could only see his face when the lights were dimmed. Immediately, we began to see faces. I guided the kids to sing and call out to loved ones. We sang a variety of fun holiday songs, hooting and ad-libbing where we saw fit.

We could see my husband's face change and a few times asked if he had opened his eyes. This was the beginning of the energy shift and we were beginning to notice spirit faces with eyes opening and a variety of facial expressions. One of the spirit personalities tilted his head and held an expression with an open mouth and eyes. He looked back and forth over the small crowd and smiled as he transfixed his gaze upon our daughter's fiancé. This was a completely new experience for our kids and their partners as the ones present had never seen spirit before.

It became apparent that this spirit was looking straight at the fiancé and wouldn't look away. I began to ask him if the spirit looked like anyone he knew. His first response was an adamant, "No." But as the spirit face continued to look directly at him and smile, I said, "This has to be for you. Are you sure you don't recognize him?"

After a moment, he responded. "Well, it does look exactly like my uncle who recently passed away." And as soon as he realized what he had said, he gasped with emotion and became silent. His response was very unexpected and surprised even him. I reached out to make sure he was okay as the room was too dark to see him standing beside me. He was verbally non-responsive and I didn't know whether or not he would faint. We decided to bring the lights up slowly so we could verify that he was okay.

Afterward, we discussed the experience. He had some conflicting beliefs due to the way he was raised and didn't know what to think of it all. I explained how spirit sometimes comes through for us because we need to know they are okay. And sometimes, they come through to us so we can let someone else know that they are okay. He had been thinking of other family members and wondered if this experience would bring peace to them.

If someone has never seen spirit before, this experience can be quite startling. We learned that standing is probably not the best way to view a transfiguration and in future sittings, we always provided enough chairs for everyone. Although this was a shockingly new experience for him, it was undoubtedly validated.

Arthur Conan Doyle

One night, we had some friends visiting and decided to demonstrate transfiguration. I sat for the group while my daughter was the designated light controller. Three friends were present, two of which were sisters.

As the lights were dimmed, the group began singing. I remember how joyful the room felt as the beautiful, fun notes filled the air, pumping it with energy. They sang "Row, Row, Row Your Boat," "Twinkle Twinkle Little Star," and "You Are My Sunshine." The laughter was filled with anticipation for what they were about to witness.

My face began to shift immediately, and the group first saw familiar historical faces. I had silently called in Abe Lincoln and George Washington because I knew that they would be easily recognizable. The group gasped when they saw both presidents and identified them right away.

There was a beautiful dark-haired woman who appeared more than once and lingered for a long time. She was described as having a joyful presence and wore colorful clothes. One sitter saw her full-body apparition as she danced around, moving her body and both arms. The sitter felt that this was an ancestor spirit of hers, though she didn't know her in this lifetime.

The sitters clearly saw the creator of Sherlock Holmes, Arthur Conan Doyle, who was someone that I felt a connection to. My house had a guest suite named in his honor. None of the attendees knew that just a few days prior I had my own spirit interaction with him. As I carefully selected décor to match the era and theme of his life, I found a photo of Arthur Conan Doyle standing beside his friend and nemesis Houdini. The day I discovered their odd friendship, I laughed and considered not putting that photo in the room. Houdini was known to disrepute the work of mediums—not so much because he didn't believe in the afterlife or want to but because there were many fraudulent mediums in operation at the time. His own quest to connect with his beloved mother after her passing sent him into the underbelly of all matter of mediumship. Due to his own frustration of not feeling reconnected to his departed mother, he set out on a quest to prove all mediumship as fraud.

Arthur Conan Doyle was a wonderful supporter of mediumship and Spiritualism, which caused the infamous clash. As I trimmed the photo to fit the frame, I contemplated if it would be okay to hang it in his room or not. Just then, the sound of a ringing bell went off behind me. When I turned to look, I discovered that my bell had been thrown off my bookcase and landed on the floor a few feet away. There was nothing beside it to make it fall as it rested comfortably on the glass shelf near the back wall of my bookcase, where it had been for years. I paused for a moment wondering if hanging this photo would cause a conflicting energy in the house. But after reflection, I felt that the bell was not a warning but rather an affirmation and I immediately felt a kind and understanding energy that accompanied it.

No doubt, I was picking up on the energy of Arthur Conan Doyle, as I believe he did not hold any bad feelings against Houdini. This made me smile and I continued to frame and then hang the photo in the guest room. The attendees knew nothing about my flying bell or that I suspected Arthur was spending time in our house, helping me with my own journey of mediumship. His physical presence during the transfiguration confirmed my feelings and I was happy that he was still visiting.

The two sisters who were sitting that day had lost their father a couple of years prior. The father appeared three to four times, looking back and forth until finally setting his gaze upon the younger sister. Both girls were thrilled to see him again and knew that his spirit was silently conveying a message of love and protection that needed to be received.

When the sister's grandma appeared, it literally took the elder sister's breath away. She mentioned wanting to get up and touch her because she appeared with such clarity.

We had so much fun and experienced reconnection and healing with spirit. I believe that the transfiguration was a success due to the high vibration of love shared between all parties present and the joyful optimism the sitters held.

Happy Birthday

We had friends over and decided to demonstrate transfiguration for them. My husband, daughter, and I all took turns sitting for our friends. We began by singing upbeat songs that we all knew and spirit began to show themselves immediately. The first recognizable face was Abe Lincoln. His prominent nose and detailed top hat made him easy to recognize. I had to chuckle because he is undoubtedly the most common spirit that comes through for us during demonstrations. I don't know if it's because he is one of our favorite presidents, or if it is because he was so open minded about séances while he was living. Whatever the case, he seems to be a regular visitor during transfigurations.

One of our friends felt the entire room fill up with a comforting energy that she associated with her previous fiancé in spirit. Her entire body felt a slight pressure as if she were being hugged. She saw partial transfiguration of his face upon the medium but the entire experience was beyond where the medium was sitting. She felt his presence everywhere and this allowed her to feel reconnected with her loved one and know that he was okay.

Our other friend saw and felt his father and grandfather before the energy began to wane. We began singing again, and as we ran out of songs, introduced the "happy birthday" song to our encore. We sang happy birthday a few times as we interjected the names of those present. Suddenly, the audience gasped and said that they saw Marilyn Monroe appear transfigured over my face. Her entire image had shown through, with pouty lips, bombshell hair, and the signature mole. She literally turned her head and winked one eye as she blew a kiss to the crowd. Perhaps it was the birthday song that evoked her presence, reminding her of her own rendition when she sang, "Happy Birthday, Mr. President."

Our friends were new to this experience and undoubtedly had their reservations. They presumed it would be scary and/or dangerous due to the misrepresentation of mainstream media on the topic. They were relieved to discover that it was a fun and lighthearted experience. They were able to reconnect with their loved ones in a meaningful way and experience their soul survival through visual transfiguration, as well as feeling and sensing their presence. They also mentioned that they felt entirely safe the whole time and that this was a beneficial experience for them.

six

Other Techniques for Spirit Communication

Sensory Deprivation

There are a variety of techniques that use sensory deprivation to assist the stillness of mind to enhance more subtle, psychic abilities and may indeed be the opening into the spirit world you seek. The psychomanteum, floatation tank, and ganzfeld effect can all be utilized for sensory deprivation and may help with a greater understanding of how spiritual energy is perceived. These techniques are known to increase intuitive abilities by slowing the brain waves and may be helpful for those seeking to connect with the spirit world.

Psychomanteum

The ancient Greeks used a psychomanteum to connect with the spirit world. They built underground structures and employed the use of caves with long, dark corridors to provide for complete darkness and sensory deprivation. The passageways led to an isolated, dark cave housing a copper bowl filled with water. They would gaze into the water in hopes of seeing their deceased loved one reflected back to them. That ancient practice was so effective that it has been brought forth into current times by employing the use of darkened rooms with mirrors in a variety of homemade psychomanteums.

How to Set Up and Use a Psychomanteum at Home

It is advised to emotionally connect with your loved one in spirit before you begin. You may do this by recalling special memories, looking at photos, or talking about them to someone else. If you are alone, just thinking about them helps to connect you to their energy. Try to recall happy memories because the joy and love will be easy to transmit into the spirit world and enhance the ability of spirit to come through.

Sit comfortably in a chair that is facing a large wall mirror in a darkened room. Make sure your neck is not strained and that you can see the entire mirror by facing it straight on. The mirror should be hanging at the appropriate height. One small candle may be lit beside you so that you can faintly make out a reflection in the mirror. Sit and gaze into the mirror as you allow your thoughts to drift. This process may take time as your mind relaxes and you are able to enter stillness of thought. Some people experience numbing of arms and tingling of fingers while others report that images of a cloud-like substance can be seen in the mirror.

Many people experience the presence of their loved ones, either as a reflection in the mirror or an image that they associate with their loved one. The image could be anything that you associate with your loved one or a symbol that they have used to help you identify them. Sometimes, the candle will flicker and alert you to spirit presence entering the room, while at times, it may even be blown out. Just be open to any subtle feelings and impressions you get while you sit and scry into the mirror. This process could take up to an hour and may take more than one sitting, depending on your ability to quiet your mind.

Dr. Raymond Moody is referred to as the father of near-death experience and has compiled a book about psychomanteum experiences called *Reunions*. He advises writing down any impressions, visions, and experiences immediately following the session.

Floatation Tank

The floatation tank was developed in 1954 by John Lilly, a medical practitioner who studied sensory deprivation and its effects on mental health. The original floatation tanks were called isolation tanks or chambers and included a full-body immersion in water. Thanks to some forward-thinking health spas, the floatation tanks have become more accessible in the United States. The new flotation pods are filled with Epsom salts that keep the client afloat as they drift off into alpha and theta brainwave relaxed states. The Epsom salts keep the client's body buoyant, which allows for deeper relaxation. Perhaps it is because it reminds us of the womb that the circular, warm pod seems to create a nurturing experience and is so beneficial for healing, meditation, problem-solving, and relaxation. Although the health spas offer a variety of colored lights and nature sounds to enhance the session, if you are seeking spirit communication it may be best to recreate the sensory deprivation experience with complete darkness.

I would advise trying the floatation tank both in silence and with relaxing nature sounds. Whichever brings you to a place of inner peace will be more effective. However, sometimes, the music or nature sounds could inadvertently drown out a disembodied spirit voice.

How to Create the Floatation Experience at Home

You may use a common bathtub for an at-home floatation experience. Begin with a hot bath containing about a cup of Epsom salts. It is recommended to keep the water at waist height as you sit in the tub, with your upper body outside of the water but relaxing against the tub wall. It may be helpful to read a book until your eyes begin to feel tired or relaxed. Falling asleep in the bathtub is not advised; however, you may relax into a light, meditative state for this experience. It is best to attempt this when there is someone else nearby that can check on you.

Next, ask spirit to make themselves known or ask for a loved one in spirit to communicate with you. As you relax, you will become more receptive to spirit and the water makes an excellent conductor for spirit energy. If you have the shower curtain pulled closed, the energy will be able to build in the bathing stall, similar to the cabinet that spiritualists use for demonstrating physical mediumship.

It is possible to receive spirit communication while bathing, both in the tub and the shower. I have received mental mediumship in the form of thoughts and images in my mind but have also physically seen spirit and heard audible spirit voices while bathing. My family used to joke that all I had to do was go take a shower and I would come out with some sort of epiphany or validation from the spirit world.

Once the contact is made, you may continue to feel the spirit presence until you re-engage with your regular routine. Stillness of mind creates the opening that our loved ones seek, making it easier for them to connect with us.

Ganzfeld Effect

The ganzfeld effect is a sensory deprivation experiment used to induce spirit communication. It is drawn from the experience of not being able to see during extreme whiteout conditions caused by snowstorms.

When a person's eyes are open and have nothing physical to focus on, the vision often expands to see things that are less perceivable at other times. While some people claim this is a sort of hallucination, others acknowledge that part of seeing the spiritual world includes releasing the ability to only see the physical one, even if just for a split second.

Here's How to Have Your Own Ganzfeld Experiment at Home

You can easily try this experiment at home. Cut a ping-pong ball in half and tape each half over your eyes so that both are covered. You could also spray paint goggles with frosted white paint. (Several coats of spray paint may be required to ensure an opaque quality to the goggles). The objective with either technique is to keep your eyes open but not be able to see anything.

Once your eyes are covered, you may sit in silence or listen to white noise. The white noise is often helpful to produce spirit voices and may enhance your experience. White noise is available on audio CD, or may be achieved by adjusting a radio just slightly off a station. You may also turn your television to a channel that doesn't come in. Static or white noise is what you will need, so refrain from listening to music or human dialogue. It is suggested to aim a red light (red flashlight works fine) toward your face.

You will notice an increased awareness in hearing right away. It may take a few minutes before you begin to notice subtle energies moving about the room. This technique can help you to heighten your awareness of spirit presence and learn what it feels like to be in the company of spirit. This experiment requires trust in your environment and trust in those who help you do it. I do suggest that you have at least one person sitting beside you as a sort of control. They will sit silently and not move—but they can provide a sort of protection from others who may enter the room, curious pets, or supernatural occurrences. They can also write down anything that you tell them so you can enjoy the full experience and then review the notes later.

The control should write down the time that things occur. If the person doing the experiment says that they feel someone walking behind them, the control should write it down along with a time stamp. (Such as: 3:16—feels like someone walking behind me.) Be sure to notice sounds, smells, and any feelings or sensations as well. Write it all down. You may do this experiment for twenty minutes or so. If you have not sustained heightened senses or altered states of consciousness for long durations before, this can make you feel a little tired afterward. You will get used to this the more you do it. You will also become better at expanding your energy beyond your personal space, allowing you to become more receptive to spirit energy.

Brain Hemispheres & Energy

What does the brain have to do with mediumship, scrying, and transfiguration? Perhaps a better understanding of how the brain relates to mediumship and heightened states of awareness will aid you in your development and ability to see spiritually.

The hemispheres of the brain are associated with logic or creativity. Through the use of a brain scan, scientists can now verify that mediumship/channeling happens in the right hemisphere of the brain. If you have ever watched a medium convey a message from spirit, they will often look up to the right as if retrieving information from someone standing to their side. I have often experienced this exact occurrence while channeling a message from spirit. I became aware that the receptivity to information from spirit was somehow coming through on the right portion of my brain and while concentrating on what was being said, looking up to the right seems to help me "tune in" better.

While the right hemisphere is somehow activated during mediumship, it is thought that the highest form of brain performance comes from being brain balanced, or using both hemispheres equally. Leonardo da Vinci and Mozart were known to be brain balanced. The absent-minded genius Albert Einstein was also known to be brain balanced. Brain balanced individuals can be creative, musical, and daydreamy, followed by amazing feats of genius. It seems that they allow their left brain (critical thinking) time off, while somehow allowing their right brain to be stimulated, thereby heightening the facilities of both hemispheres. Albert Einstein claimed to "receive" his greatest ideas for invention and theory through mediation. Some would even say that he was tapping into his own mediumistic or channeling ability.

In the late 1950s, neurofeedback was introduced as a study of consciousness. It was discovered that people could learn to alter their own brain activity through what is called sensory motor rhythm (SMR). NASA used biofeedback and SMR in their training of astronauts and it is now used widely to help students develop the focus needed for learning, to control epilepsy, and create brain balance. This indicates that anyone can learn to utilize the part of their brain associated with mediumship and create more brain balance.

If you feel that you have a tendency for left brain dominance, there are things you can do to help activate the right hemisphere or to become more brain balanced. One thing you can practice is visualization. In other words, your brain holds the key that allows you to access the spirit world.

Indigenous tribes from around the world probably didn't know much about the brain but they did know how to access the spirit world. Ironically, some of their simple techniques are found to stimulate the area of the brain that increases their ability to connect with spirit (aka, the right hemisphere).

Whether you attempt brain balance or increased activation of the right hemisphere, the following exercises may be helpful for you.

Shamanic Spinning

A good friend of mine took me into the woods and taught me how to do the shamanic spin. She had been taught by a Native American shaman still practicing traditional healing and ancestor communication. At first, I thought it was too simple to work. I questioned how such a simple thing like spinning could help bring about a spirit connection. I did as she said … and amazingly, it worked.

How To Do the Shamanic Spin

Make sure you are in a large clearing so that you will not run into any structure or foliage. Have an intention of what you would like to receive. You may ask for guidance to a question you have about life or you may wish to communicate with a deceased loved one. Hold your intention as you begin this process.

Standing with your arms straight out to each side, close your eyes and spin in circles as fast as you can. It really helps to have a few people hold the perimeter to prevent you from running into anything. Spin and spin as fast as you can until your legs give out. Allow your body to fall gently to the ground and then lay still where you fall. As you lay there, allow your mind to drift. Be receptive to any images, thoughts, sounds, or sensations around you. With your eyes remaining closed, you may see visions or feel spirit approach you. Just be receptive, knowing you are safe and that the people you have selected to aid you are worthy of your trust. (Make sure they are.)

Ancient Shaman from all parts of the world have used spinning to help gain access to the spirit world as it is associated with out-of-body experiences. Along with spinning, rhythmic dancing, chanting, and drumming are helpful aids to connect with the spirit world. These simple procedures help to activate the right brain and can actually induce a theta brainwave, making you more receptive to the subtle energy of spirit.

Left and Right Brain Activation

Many modern-day mediums know how important it is to activate the left and right hemisphere of the brain for mediumship.

How to Activate Both Hemispheres

This can be achieved through gently shaking your head from left to right as if tilting from shoulder to shoulder slightly.

Some mediums have been noted for clicking a pen in their left hand and then the right hand at opposing intervals.

There are many ways that this brain balancing can be achieved—clicking your fingers, or by following a light back and forth as with Induced After Death Communications (IADC). (*Induced After Death Communication*, developed by author Allan L. Botkin, Psy.D.) This technique has been used clinically to help countless veterans suffering from wartime trauma to find healing. It is a technique taught to help individuals access their own visions and communication with deceased loved ones and is administered by trained professionals. There is much to learn from all techniques and finding the right formula to enhance your own abilities will allow you to see spiritually with more ease.

Energy and Auras

Knowing about your own energy field can really assist you in connecting with spirit. When you become aware of your own energy, you will know when the energy in the room changes, indicating a spirit presence. You will also be able to tell by the energy signature who the spirit is or who he/she is there to communicate with. Your energy is unique and carries with it subtle clues to your character and personality. When you pass, your energy will still be felt the same way as it did when you were living.

Learn to Feel Energy Signatures

You may practice this technique by asking a living loved one to enter the room when your eyes are closed. Pay attention to the feeling in the room and any new emotions you become aware of. You may also notice subtle scents or odors associated with the loved one. Ask yourself how your own energy is affected by the close proximity. You may find that some people are more difficult to detect if they resonate similar to you; this often happens with family members or close friends who have a lot in common.

You will notice that the more you do this, the better you will become at figuring out who is entering the room before you actually see them. This is the same way it works with the spirit world. If you currently don't know much about energy, it would be helpful to take some classes. This alone may really help you advance in your work with the spirit world.

Opening Chakras

One of the most helpful techniques you should do prior to engaging in spirit communication or any type of psychic or healing work is to open and balance your chakras.

How to Open and Balance Your Chakras

The process is simple and works. Sit comfortably with both feet flat on the ground in front of you. Keep your arms straight at your side or resting upon your lap (not crossed). Close your eyes and imagine that you are sending your own energy down into the ground, deep into Mother Earth. Allow your energy to be grounded, as you imagine bringing the energy back up through the bottoms of your feet now, up through your legs and reaching the base of your spine. As the energy continues to climb upward, it will pass through each of your main seven chakras. Spend a moment at each one, meditating on it and feeling it open in perfect balance to the others. (It is most beneficial to have chakras balanced rather than having one open wide and the others rather small.)

As you imagine the energy rising, begin to witness the open and balanced chakra in the base of the spine; this is known as your root chakra. Slightly above that one is your sacral chakra (just below the belly button) and then the solar plexus (just above the belly button). Continue to imagine the energy raising into the heart chakra in the center of your chest, the throat chakra, the third eye (forehead area), and then finally, the crown chakra on top of your head.

When you have visualized this as complete, continue to move that energy up and out your crown chakra and into the heavens to connect with the Highest Power/Creator/Universe. You will notice that when you are connected above and below as all chakras are open and balanced, you will be most receptive to healing, intuitive guidance, and spirit communication. This is actually a great way to start your day each morning, keeping you in alignment with synchronicities and increased energy.

Expand the Aura

Your aura is the energy field surrounding your physical body. A person can manipulate or expand the size of their aura through meditation and intention. Spirit energy is often felt in the energy center behind your head where the skull meets the spine. There is a soft spot just below the skull where spiritual energy resides. This area is called the medulla oblongata and is often referred to as "the mouth of god," "jade pillow," or "golden chalice." Taoists regard this point as a storage area for extra energy and believe it receives information from spirit, often working as an antenna bringing forth spirit communication. It is an area receptive to universal knowledge, cosmic energy, and wisdom as it connects to the crown chakra, which is also known for divine connection.

As you work with your ability to communicate with spirit, it may be helpful to expand your aura behind you to allow spirit energy to enter the medulla oblongata. Most people tend to keep their aura tucked in close to their body as a sense of protection, especially on the back side.

How to Expand Your Aura

During this exercise, you will intend that your aura move out further behind you, knowing that you are safe to do this. Sit comfortably in a chair with feet flat on the floor and hands resting by your side. Close your eyes. Take a few deep breaths in and then gently blow the air out through pursed lips. Relax as you visualize yourself in a bubble of protection. Your aura is the bubble of protection and you can expand it at will. Continue breathing as you imagine that the energy field behind you is now moving farther out from your body. Expand your field to four feet or farther.

Imagine that you are opening the medulla oblongata and balancing the energy in harmony with your chakras. Breathe in and out a few times. Allow energy to come in through this energy center and be receptive to any new images, ideas, or direct messages.

As you explore energy, auras, and activating the hemispheres of the brain through these techniques, you will heighten your receptivity to spirit. Remember that this is a sacred journey but may also be a fun and enjoyable one. Spirit loves laughter and being in joy can really help increase your success.

seven

Signs from Spirit

When I have finished doing mediumship, teaching a class, or demonstrating transfiguration, I advise people to ask for their own signs from the spirit world. This can be an important step in helping people to connect with the spirit world so they can build their own relationship with the other side. If they have connected with a loved one, I will tell my clients to ask spirit for a sign to confirm the message they received. Without fail, my clients always tell me that they received validation.

Signs from the spirit world can be anything that is interpreted as having to do with the loved one in spirit. It could be that a song plays on the radio every time you think of your loved one. You may be sent pennies from heaven or other gifts from spirit that seemingly just appear out of nowhere. Spirit will use your dreams to send you messages and may show you a significant item that you associate with them, such as their favorite food, type of car, hobby, or color. You may receive a whiff of a certain scent like cigar smoke or cologne that reminds you of your loved one. It is possible for spirit to send you thoughts, which will usually be repetitive until you realize that the thoughts are not your own. You may get a physical sensation, a warming heart, a tingly feeling, or an actual touch from spirit. You may begin to get daily visits from a certain animal or see a dragonfly each time you reflect upon them. Birds are especially noted for bringing messages from the spirit world.

Hawk and Raven

One time, a client drove four hours to have a private session with me in person. Right when she arrived, she remarked that two birds had accompanied her on the entire drive. She knew that it was a sign from the spirit world but did not know what it meant. She was asking that her recently departed son come through during our session together so she would know he was okay. She also wanted confirmation that I was the right person to have the session with. When I asked her what type of birds had led her to my house, her answer didn't surprise me. She said one was a hawk and one was a raven. I found that interesting indeed because those are both my animal totems that routinely show up when I ask for signs or help from the spirit world.

I first became aware that the hawk was my totem about fifteen years ago. There isn't a day that the hawk misses his visit and it doesn't matter where I live or where I am traveling. In fact, the hawk was noticed by everyone around me for years before I finally acknowledged his daily presence. Hawk totem relates to intuition and higher chakras. Hawk brings wisdom, spiritual awareness, and a higher perspective. When I look back at when the hawk first began appearing daily to me, it coincided with my spiritual gifts opening up wide.

The raven began coming to me about six years ago, and I was much more in tune with my surroundings by that time. When I finished building the medicine wheel at my house, I left to run a quick errand and upon return, saw four large ravens sitting beside the medicine wheel as if they were having a conversation about it. Medicine wheels are used by many ancient cultures, including most Native American tribes; the meaning of the different directions within the circle vary from tribe to tribe but the wheel is primarily used for healing. I selected the land because of the high vibration it contained and was told that it was once used for Native American rituals of healing.

I used my dowsing rods to determine the highest energetic point and that became the center of my wheel, as well as the fire pit. The burning of the fire was also significant in that it would release energy back into the heavens. I dug out a perimeter and filled it with small river rocks, marking each direction (north, south, east, and west) with a tiki torch. Under each directional signifier, I buried crystals (Herkimer diamond) to activate a light grid within the wheel. Through meditation and intention, I infused the medicine wheel with the ability to maintain a light portal that would help bring lost souls to the light.

I sat in my car and watched the ravens for quite a while. They seemed to be chatting with each other about my medicine wheel as they overlooked the project. After observing their interactions, I felt that they were pleased and that they were well aware of the purpose that the wheel would serve.

The raven is associated with taking souls to heaven and they often become totem animals for people who work with the spirit world and convey messages of healing. People who have no fear of the dark and who bring light are compatible with raven. They represent magic, rebirth, and healing. When they were finished examining my medicine wheel, they took their places in the tall trees above it. Since that time, they have been more present in my life and are often alerting me to potential harm and upcoming life changes.

When my client told me of her unlikely chaperones that accompanied her on her long drive to my house, and quite literally, right to my house … I was not surprised. I explained that the hawk and raven are both my totem animals and that brought a comforted, large smile to her face. This validation was for her but it was also for me. She had been asking if I was going to be able to help her and had prayed for a sign. Having the hawk and raven lead her to me was something that I had not encountered before.

I am constantly in awe of how amazing the spirit world is and how they can help bring people together for healing. This experience also confirmed to me how supported I was in doing my healing work.

Fly-fishing Hook

Another time, I was called to send healing to a distant family member. He contacted me to inquire about my work with the spirit world. At the time, I was still involved with para-normal investigations and was very active in the field. Something stood out in his message when I became aware that he needed help but may not have wanted to ask me.

I usually don't get involved with other people's lives un-less asked to or spirit tells me to, so I tried to let it go. I left my computer and went downstairs to let the dog outside and upon my return, found something on my desk that wasn't there before. As I mentioned before, a physical item that ap-pears is known as an apport or a gift from the spirit world. I saw it immediately but didn't know what it was. As I came closer to the desk, I could make out a small black feather with a hook. Still, I had no idea what it was. No one was upstairs or had access to my office. My husband was out of town. But somehow, this item manifested itself on top of my desk where there was no chance it would be missed. I called for my daughter and we admired the tiny feathered hook as we googled the description to find out what it was. *Ah ha*, a fly-fishing hook. I had never seen one before. I had no idea why I had received a fly-fishing hook from spirit but knew that it was related to my relative. I took this as a confirmation to go ahead and send healing to him.

I sat quietly in my Victorian chair, surrounded by candles and crystals while I connected to a place in time where his soul was in turmoil. I began to clear energy, trauma, and soul fragments given to the land during battle. There were others near him in spirit that needed to be healed so I worked with them to find the light. As the black energy began to clear, I saw enough white light around my relative to notice that he was accompanied by some ancestors in spirit. I recognized my grandpa Palm right away. He was showing me that he was there with him and that he was the one that guided me to help him.

Afterward, I contacted my relative and told him that I was given a gift from the spirit world but could not tell how it fit in. When I told him what the item was, he mentioned that he had just taken fly-fishing lessons a month earlier. I asked if he was aware that Grandpa was with him in spirit and he said yes. He said that he feels Grandpa around him all the time and was actually talking about him when he was taking his fly-fishing lessons. I could definitely confirm that Grandpa was with him and aware of what he was going through. I had literally seen Grandpa's spirit standing beside him like a guardian angel and knew that he was not planning to leave his side anytime soon.

I was so thankful that I was able to participate in the process of healing, and that through this, I was able to reconnect with a family member whom I loved. I know that Grandpa was very happy to have had a hand in reuniting the family.

Penny for the Bride

Sometimes the signs received from the spirit world are less dramatic. They are nonetheless just as meaningful. Some very close friends of mine came to get married at our Victorian house and neither bride nor groom had their father with them. They had both passed away years earlier, but the general feeling was that they would show up in spirit to offer their love and support for the nuptials.

We had planned to have the wedding outside on the lawn, but just as the time came for the wedding it began to rain very hard. I made a very quick decision to move the folding chairs into the carriage house where we could create a makeshift altar and perform the ceremony under cover. The boys gathered the folding chairs and quickly hurried across the yard to set up.

Everyone wondered how we would pull this off and shuffled around to accommodate the new arrangement. The bride was with me and we were the last ones still remaining in the house when I picked up the candle stand to carry outside. Just then, we heard the sound of metal hitting the hardwood floor with a couple bounces and then a roll. When we turned to look we saw a penny coming toward us as if it had been thrown in our direction from across the room.

Right away, the bride knew this to be a sign from her father and had all the validation that she needed. He had been sending her pennies from heaven since he had passed away, and she knew he had made it to her wedding after all.

Many people are familiar with pennies from heaven as gifts sent from the spirit world. It doesn't have to be a penny; it could be any kind of coin. This is just one way spirit has of telling you that they are still with you and that they love you.

Yellow

On the anniversary of my little sister's passing I feel her spirit around me. Our birthdays were only six days apart so we often celebrated our birthdays together. I always think of her on her birthday and do something special to send my love to her in the spirit world. Sometimes I buy her roses and sometimes I bake cupcakes in her honor. I also commemorate the day of her passing.

On this particular anniversary, I was sitting in my office alone and I became aware that she was standing beside me. I opened the drawer of my desk and retrieved my spirit box device and my digital recorder. I turned both on at the same time and asked one question. I said, "Mary, if this is you, can you please tell me what color vehicle we drove to your funeral?" About one second later, her voice spoke to me through the SB-7 spirit box. She said, "Yellow?" I was thrilled that she was able to make clear contact and bring forward her voice. It was not only her voice, but the inflection of how she spoke was easy to validate as well as the correct answer. We had driven a forty-foot-long racing coach to her out-of-town funeral to help offer sleeping accommodations for ourselves and other family, and it was painted corvette yellow. That's all I needed to hear.

I turned the recorder and spirit box off and I smiled with happy tears in my eyes. I often share that recording in my afterlife presentations because it is so clear and meaningful.

Civil War Ghost

Sometimes I feel spirit around me and don't know who they are right away. I was visiting a civil war battlefield with my husband, daughter, and parents when a ghost tried to make contact with me. We were at the Battle of the Crater in Virginia and just as we left the car, I told my husband to turn the digital recorder on. My family were the only people present at the battlefield so I knew we would not have any contamination from the voices of other tourists.

We walked to the middle of the battlefield where an old brick structure was erected. It appeared to be a two-story house with two fireplaces, but there was no sign to describe the significance of the structure. The entire park was well marked so I thought it was odd that this structure was not. The Union soldiers had set up camp on the hill by the brick structure and the Confederate troops were on the opposite hill to the south, where the Battle of the Crater actually took place.

We walked across the park and as we entered the area beside the crater, I felt something rub against my pant leg near my ankle. It was autumn so the weather was cool and I was wearing long jeans with boots that laced up. The feeling of my ankle being touched was very apparent, so I presumed that my boot had come untied. I handed my purse to my husband as I bent down to check my shoelace. As I lifted my pant leg, I noticed that my boot was still tied in a perfectly tight bow, and I said, "Oh, it's still tied." Just after that, a female spirit said, "It almost come undone." The voice could not be heard by our own ears but was recorded in perfect clarity.

It took me by surprise that I would encounter a helpful female spirit on the battlefield when I presumed that any spirit I made contact with would be a civil war soldier. I have a feeling that she belonged to the family that owned the brick house and was misplaced when the Union confiscated the hill for battle. I did some research on the property after we returned home and found out that it was in the same family for a long time and there were some daughters who lived there during the war.

Funeral Cat

One of my friends owned and operated a haunted bed and breakfast in Minnesota. When visiting the historic property, guests were always greeted by her enormously large and friendly coon cats. Tennessee and Miss Sadie were known to prowl the property, knocking on guest rooms and offering snuggles to the guests. My friend taught classes on ghosts, did healing work and palm readings, and hosted murder mystery dinner parties. I loved visiting her inn and taking part in whatever activities she had going on.

When I got word that my friend passed away, I immediately thought about her cats in the hope that someone close to her would take custody of them. She loved her cats very much and they were loyal companions to her. For some reason, I couldn't get her cats off my mind.

Days later, I attended her funeral with my daughter. It was a beautiful little gathering with heartfelt testimonials about her life and how much she would be missed. One of her friends broke into song and captivated the crowd with his angelic voice, possessing the type of sass that my friend enjoyed most.

During the entire eulogy, I kept hearing a cat meow. At first, I thought that one of her friends must have brought her cats to the funeral home so that they could go home with someone afterward. I was relieved to know that someone was helping to look after the cats for her. At times, the meows were so loud that I thought one of the cats must have gotten out of the cage and was wandering around the funeral home. It sounded like the meows went from left to right and back again by the double-hung exit door behind me. I even said something to my daughter and shared how happy I was that the cats had come to the funeral so they could go to a new home and that they were not forgotten in the bed and breakfast.

As the funeral wound down, everyone gathered in the hall. That's when I asked someone who had taken custody of the cats. They seemed surprised at my question. I mentioned that I heard her cat pacing back and forth, meowing throughout the service. The gentleman smiled as he informed me that Miss Sadie had passed right after our friend did. The other cat had found a home with a close friend. I guess Miss Sadie came to the funeral to accompany her loving companion home to heaven and to have one final chance to say goodbye to us, her friends and previous guests at the inn.

After the funeral, I was contacted by a mutual friend who stated that she had some healing dolls that she thought our friend would want me to have. We split our friend's doll collection in half and I set mine high up on the bookshelf in my healing room (just as our friend had them in her healing room). I was removing wallpaper, so the entire room was empty except for the bookcase and the dolls. It felt like there was another presence in the room with me, but I kept peeling wallpaper and didn't even turn to look.

All of a sudden, something was thrown toward me from across the room. It landed on the hardwood floor so it bounced a few times before it landed. I picked it up and didn't even know what the item was or where it had come from. It appeared to be a black cap to something, about the size of a coin. I turned to look around the room, up at the ceiling, and then, finally, the bookshelf.

I immediately laughed to myself as I honed in on the dolls, determining that this was the direction the item came from and knew this to be a sign from my friend. My friend who passed was known to be a trickster and had a spry sense of humor. I felt that she was acknowledging that I had her dolls and she was pleased. I still have her dolls but they haven't thrown anything since that time.

Blueberry Pie

It was summer and my daughter had just graduated from high school. We were invited to attend one of her best friend's graduation parties. We had been friends with their family since our girls were in scouts together. As I showered, my mind began to wander and I thought about how well the graduate had turned out. She was smart and beautiful and so talented. She could sing like a songbird and came from a loving family. Then suddenly I thought, *I wonder how she grew so tall?* Both her parents were shorter in stature than she was, so I wondered who had that tall gene in their family.

It was just a random thought and I didn't think much of it. Then I closed my eyes to rinse the shampoo out of my hair when all of a sudden, I intuitively saw a blueberry pie. There was no doubt as to what kind of pie it was, so I must have been given the knowing along with the image. *What possible significance could blueberry pie have?* I wondered.

When I emerged from the shower, I emailed her mother to ask if blueberry pie meant anything special to her. She told me that her grandmother, whom she was very close to and loved very much, used to bake pie for everyone's birthday. Year after year, she baked her pies and everyone in the family had a favorite that she would bake specifically for them. She told me with tears in her eyes that her special pie was always blueberry. This simple message brought her peace and joy because she knew that her grandmother was going to be present for her daughter's graduation party and that somehow, she was baking a special pie in heaven for her. As it turned out, the tall gene did come from that side of the family and her grandmother was quite proud about stepping up to claim it.

———

The more aware you are, the more signs you will become aware of. You have probably been receiving signs from the spirit world your entire life but didn't know it. Once you begin to identify what type of signs certain spirits send you, it will be easier to discern who is around you.

Everyone has ancestors in spirit who are excited to be part of their life, even though they died before you were born. You could have great-great grandparents hanging out with you and not even know it. Why? They are invested in their offspring. They love you and want to help you.

The more you open up to the spirit world, the more help you can receive from it. Spend some time getting to know your spirit team and what they help you with. You can do this by doing some family genealogy, and make sure to include your friends (old and new), teachers, lovers, and pets. Everyone you encounter in life can choose to be with you in spirit after they pass. Most people only think of close family as coming to visit—but it could be anyone. Remember, we all have a purpose for being here and everyone who interacts with you is part of your path in some way.

eight

Space Clearing

When you have completed scrying, transfiguring, or any other kind of mediumship work, it is important to clear your energy and space. While the spirit world is around you at all times, a portal is opened to the spirit world each time you engage it. Think of it as a bridge that connects you to the spirit world, allowing communication and energies to move between the physical plane and spirit world. At the end of a session, you should clear your energy and space and intentionally close the door to the portal.

Once, when I was connecting to a recently departed in spirit, I left the connection open to receive further guidance while I prepared for my day. As I went to shower, the spirit actually entered the shower stall with me, appearing as a gray mass of energy. I both saw and felt the spirit energy, just as I began to get clear pictures in my mind's eye and intuitively hear the exact words for a message. To say this surprised me is an understatement.

With experience comes respect for boundaries. I now clear off my energy and space each time I am done so that the spirit world does not infiltrate my daily life with family.

If you forget to close a session, you could inadvertently invite all sorts of spirits to enter your home and life. Depending on your awareness and ability to discern spirit energy, this could be a detriment. Oftentimes, a medium can attract unfavorable spirits who are unhealed or wish to interfere and cause havoc for the living. If this happens, you will notice that you feel drained in energy or may become moody or even depressed. When a spirit is in your space for too long, it is using your energy field to sustain itself on this plane. For that reason, it is very important to set your own boundaries and keep your energy intact. Knowing that you can connect at any time helps eliminate the desire to always stay connected.

As a medium, you deserve time off!

Remember, not all spirits are loved ones, nor do they all have your highest and best interest at heart. Next time you walk into a crowded room, look around and assess the crowd. Would you feel comfortable inviting all those living people into your personal space and home? Think of the spirit world as a crowded room of living people. After you have been of service, provided loving connections between the living and the spirit world, empty the room and reclaim your space.

How to Clear Space

Close your eyes and imagine that you are going to that place of highest connection with Creator/God. You are comfortable and relaxed as you connect your energy into Mother Earth to ground you. Imagine that you are bringing up energy from Mother Earth through the bottom of your feet, up through your entire body, opening and balancing each chakra on the way up to the top of your head. Allow that energy to go out the top of your crown chakra and out into the universe to connect with the energy of all creation. Hold the intention that you are connecting to Creator/God. (This is very important to bring your energy to the highest level and to allow you to work with divine energy). You may still call upon all your guides and ascended masters to assist you once you have this connection. When you feel connected, you will notice a calming energy that radiates light and unconditional love. You may see sparkles here too.

Here is what you can say to clear the space:

"It is commanded to clear this space of any residual energy, clearing myself, the sitters, and the space. Release any unhealed emotions and attachments. Bring healing to any spirits present, while sending any spirits in need of healing to the light. Allow pure, unconditional love to fill the hearts and minds of all present, including those in spirit. Thank you."

Once this (or something similar) is said, maintain your meditative state and wait until the process is complete. You may sense or feel energy leaving the room, a rush of gratitude from spirit or just a feeling that it is complete.

You may burn sage or cedar to help clear the space. Ring a bell or Tibetan tingsha bells.

This process will clear the space of any emotionally charged connections as well as bring healing to both the living and spirit. At times, our loved ones pass in such a manner that they do not go into the light immediately. It is quite possible that your sitters will bring some loved ones in spirit who need a little help with the transition. If a spirit shows up who is confused, in pain, or doesn't seem healed, this process will usher them into the light and bring them healing.

Clear Negative Spirits

What happens if your sitting gets highjacked by an unwelcome spirit? If you have cleared your space and set your intention through mindful meditation or prayer, this should not happen. However, if it does, simply follow the guidelines below.

It is very important to know that negative spirits feed on fear. The more comfortable you feel about your ability to do a clearing, the better. You will discover that you and the light are much more powerful than these pesky, lower-level beings. It doesn't happen very often, especially when one has followed the protocol for protection in this book. However, sometimes, the sitters are bringing negative spirits with them. Perhaps the sitting is exactly what is needed for the spirit to be drawn out and released. That's why it is important for any medium to become acquainted and comfortable with sending negative spirits away.

If the people coming to your sittings seem to bring an assortment of negative spirits, it is your opportunity to send them away to provide the healing that the sitters seek. You could also request that your sitters spend time in meditation or prayer prior to coming so that they will arrive with clearer energy.

Release all judgment about how the negative spirits came into the room or who they entered with. Once they are sent away, they are gone unless invited back. The medium has a very important role working as a sort of ambassador between the world of the living and the spirit world. As the medium, you will become aware of many different spirits and entities and see, hear, feel, and know what effect they are having on your clients. You may send them away.

How to Clear Negative Spirits

Close your eyes and imagine that you are going to that place of highest connection with Creator/God. You are comfortable and relaxed as you connect your energy into Mother Earth to ground you. Imagine that you are bringing up energy from Mother Earth through the bottom of your feet, up through your entire body, opening and balancing each chakra on the way up to the top of your head. Allow that energy to go out the top of your crown chakra and out into the universe to connect with the energy of all creation. Hold the intention that you are connecting to Creator/God. (This is very important to bring your energy to the highest level and to allow you to work with divine energy).

Silently, command that you know the sacred name of the entity presenting itself:

"Creator, it is commanded to know the sacred name of the entity here."

Wait until you receive a name intuitively. (It usually comes right away.) As soon as you have it, command it by name to go. This will be done silently, never repeat the name aloud:

"Creator, it is commanded to send (say the name) away and back to your light now."

Typically, you will intuitively see the entity leave in a flash of dark mist. Be aware that there may be more. Oftentimes, if a person has attracted an entity like this, there will be at least three. Look to see if there are more and command to be shown any that are hidden:

"Creator, it is commanded I be shown any hidden or unseen entities now."

If any present themselves, get their names and send them away as you did previously. Always give thanks. Close the door to the portal once you see them go back to Creator.

You should notice a shift in the room and the energy will feel clearer. This process is effective for possession and oppression as well.

Some of your clients may need this help from you so it is best to feel confident instead of fearful. This may never happen to you or anyone you know, but if it does you will be able to handle it.

Does doing spiritual work cause entity attachment? No, not usually. There are several reasons why I find it important to include in this book. It is important to know that entities and negative spirits are opportunistic. They are always looking for a way to attach to someone and cause havoc in their lives. Sometimes, they find their way to people through drugs or alcohol; it is difficult to maintain a clear space with regular use of drugs or alcohol. There are some prescription drugs that can weaken a person spiritually as well. Be advised, when people are under the influence of drugs, they most likely will have attachments. Refrain from taking any mood-altering drugs or heavy painkillers prior to or during spiritual work.

When you choose to develop your skills as a medium, you are not choosing to focus on death. In fact, you are making the choice to celebrate life. You are choosing to help validate the existence of life after physical death and to improve the life of living loved ones. Becoming a catalyst for healing is quite an honor. When you step into your mediumship with this attitude, the spirits and guides will line up to work with you. They want the same things that you do—to bring healing through connections of love.

As you move forward into your own experiences with mediumship, spiritual sight, and awareness, keep it honest, keep it pure, and be of service. This will automatically keep your ego out of the way and allow you to attract the highest guides to assist you.

appendix

Questions and Answers

Can More Than Two People
Scry to See Past Lives and Spirit?

Yes. It is possible to have one person sit in front of a group with a candle up to their face as the audience looks on. Everyone should sit in a semicircle around the person in front. In this instance, the group will all gaze upon the face of the person holding the candle.

The audience should not talk as this can decrease the energy and stop the process in its tracks. This process could go much quicker due to the amount of energy coming from all the participants in the room. You may allow approximately ten minutes for this process to occur. If you intend to give each person the opportunity to sit for the group, make sure that everyone is clearing their energy in between each sitter so that no contamination of spirit energy occurs. Always give each sitter due respect as this is a sacred practice.

Can This Process Be Done Alone?

Yes. It is possible to scry into your own face by standing in front of a mirror in a dimly lit room. You will want to stand about a foot or two away from the mirror and hold the candle between your face and the mirror. You will proceed in the same manner, by gazing in your own eyes or the bridge of your nose. Don't forget to use the protection prayer and set your intention just as you would if you were doing this with a partner. This is a fun and enlightening experience because you will be able to see all of who *you* have been in previous lifetimes as well as any ancestors or loved ones that want to communicate with you.

What If I See Something That Looks Scary?

If at any time you see an image that you feel is not from the light, stop what you are doing and perform a space clearing. In most cases, you will find that you have forgotten to set your intention or do your protection prayer before you began. Remember, the spirit world is all around us at all times. When we do this technique, we will ask to be shown what is in our highest and best. If you encounter something that seems to be scary, keep in mind that this technique has tipped you off to its presence and now you can send it away. Also, keep in mind that not all scary images are bad or dark. It is quite possible that the entity you encountered has a disturbing face because it is one that you are not familiar with. In any regard, just clear it and begin again. (See "Clear Negative Spirits" in chapter 8.)

Can a Scrying Session be Photographed?

Yes. It is best to use a digital camera and to use NO flash. You will want to use a standard point-and-shoot camera rather than a high-end one. The high-end cameras have a feature called red-eye reduction and that filter can actually block out the subtle images of spirit. If your camera has red-eye reduction, it may be turned off.

It is best to use a tripod so you can ensure the person taking the photos does not move. When you see the photographs filled with double images, spirit faces, and liquid light, you will be able to verify that it was caused by high energy and not the camera moving. It is also advised to take some before and after photographs as well as during the scrying session in order to have comparison photographs. A third person will be needed to take the photographs and they should remain quiet as well.

Remember, the room is dim with mainly the light of the candle illuminating the faces of the people scrying, so the photographer will need to be rather close for the pictures to turn out. Try to capture both faces and the candle in each frame. Experiment with this a few different ways and with a few different cameras to see which work best for you.

Will the Use of a Flash Cause Harm?

Any time mediumship or communication with spirits is being photographed, flash should not be used. The white light from the flash can stop the process abruptly and may also cause physical harm to the medium or sitters. It is sometimes acceptable to use infrared to take pictures. Though, for the most part, the results will be best by using a point-and-shoot camera with no red-eye reduction, and no flash. Lights may be turned on at the end of the session once both (or all) parties have energetically cleared off and finished scrying.

Does It Make a Difference Which Camera to Use?

Yes. Aside from the information already shared above, the camera used could make a difference in capturing results. If you have never taken spirit photos before, you may need to take a lot of photos before your camera succeeds in capturing them. The photographer in this case may be just as important as the sitters and the camera are.

The photographer should be open-minded and supportive of the process. Fear or disbelief can block results. Cameras respond to the photographer in a sort of symbiotic relationship. If the photographer is on board, the camera will be too.

Develop your relationship with the camera you will be using ahead of time or use the same camera each time you do this to improve the results. If you find that you are not achieving results with a certain camera, it may be beneficial to switch cameras and begin working with a new one. It may take time to "break in" a new camera, so be patient. The more you use the same camera, the better the results will be.

Does It Make a Difference Whom You Scry With?

Absolutely! When two mediums or powerful intuitive people sit together, the results are astounding. They already have a higher vibration due to the nature of their abilities and perhaps because of the amount of healing work they have done to acquire a clear and focused energy. However, even an untrained person can do this technique with great success. If you can quiet your mind and focus, you can do this. Some people will actually produce a more powerful energy when working together because their personal energy is more compatible or in sync. Switch partners to see who you are most compatible with for scrying.

Why Don't I See Some Spirits When They are Captured in the Photo?

The technique of scrying will train your eyes to see a broader range of frequencies, but it may take time. Using a camera can aid you in discerning what you see and also gauge your progress of seeing spiritually. If you are focused on seeing past life faces on your partner, you may miss a spirit that pops in beside them, but the camera will capture it.

Don't get discouraged. As you become more adept at seeing spiritually, you will be able to take in more of your surroundings with your peripheral vision. With practice, you will be aware of all energies that come through during a session and even have your own spontaneous spiritual sight experiences.

Will This Technique Work for Me If I Am Afraid to See Spirits?

It seldom happens that someone is prevented from seeing spirits during this technique. Most people will surprise themselves when it begins to happen and feel exhilarated instead of fearful. However, if you are a person who was raised with a fear-based religion or you carry traumas from group consciousness or a past life when you suffered for seeing spirits, then you should do some spiritual healing around that issue.

Remember, we are all that we have ever been and our soul carries full memory of all events that we have lived through in every lifetime. Many people emerging as mediums today have had to do a lot of healing around issues of imprisonment, torture, persecution, and even death for having abilities. Clearing these fears and traumas allows your soul to access more of your divine self. Any psychic blocks that you may have were created by you to protect yourself from future perceived pain. It is very important to recognize this block and work through your fear.

Release subconscious programs that are no longer needed to make you feel safe. Know that you already are safe and that you are accessing these natural abilities in divine time. If you feel you need to set up a session with someone who specializes in releasing past life traumas, do so. This will affect your life in very beneficial ways as well as allowing you to see spiritually.

Is There Anything I Can Do on My Own to Help Release Past Life Trauma and Fear of Seeing Spirits?

Yes! Affirm to yourself that it is your divine right to connect with all of creation. Meditation is very helpful for discovering hidden traumas from both past and present lives as well as helping you to release them. The Meditation to Release Trauma (chapter 2) may be a helpful tool for you as you clear out old fears. I recommend reading it out loud into a recording device so you can listen to it upon playback until you feel improvement. You may also call upon your spirit guides, angels, or loved ones in the spirit world to assist you in releasing your fear. Prayer in any form, along with chanting or intention can be beneficial.

note from the author

While working with the spirit world is fun and exciting, it has also provided me with a depth of compassion that has led to a new understanding for life. My intention in writing this book is to share the miraculous benefits and gifts of healing that come from mediumship. When you or someone you know can reconnect with a loved one in spirit, you will find comfort in knowing that life does exist after physical death. We continue to exist and we will see all of our loved ones again. To me, there could not be a more comforting thought. By using the techniques in this book, you may experience a real sense of knowing through seeing and feeling spirit, and come to the realization that they have been with you all along.

—Diana Palm

references

Botkin, Allan L. PsyD. *Induced After Death Communication: A Miraculous Therapy for Grief and Loss.* Newburyport, MA: Hampton Roads Publishing, 2014.

Hurtak, J.J. *The Book of Knowledge: Keys of Enoch, 6th Edition.* Los Gatos, CA: Academy of Future Science, 2009.

Macy, Mark. *Spirit Faces: Truth About the Afterlife.* Newburyport, MA: Weiser, 2006.

Moody, Raymond Jr., and Paul Perry. *Reunions: Visionary Encounters with Departed Loved Ones.* Ivy Press, 1994.

To view scrying and transfiguration photos, visit the author's website at www.dianapalm.com.

To Write to the Author

If you wish to contact the author or would like more information about this book, please write to the author in care of Llewellyn Worldwide Ltd., and we will forward your request. Both the author and publisher appreciate hearing from you and learning of your enjoyment of this book and how it has helped you. Llewellyn Worldwide Ltd. cannot guarantee that every letter written to the author can be answered, but all will be forwarded. Please write to:

Diana Palm
℅ Llewellyn Worldwide
2143 Wooddale Drive
Woodbury, MN 55125-2989

Please enclose a self-addressed stamped envelope for reply, or $1.00 to cover costs. If outside the USA, enclose an international postal reply coupon.

Divination

For Beginners

Reading the Past, Present & Future

SCOTT CUNNINGHAM

Divination for Beginners
Reading the Past, Present & Future
SCOTT CUNNINGHAM

Anyone can practice divination. You don't need to be psychic, or believe that a higher power controls the cards. Anyone can learn to predict the future using the methods described in this book. Learn how to choose the methods that works best for you, and ask the right questions so you get accurate answers. Discover the secrets of a wide variety of methods, from Tarot cards and the I Ching to crystal gazing, palmistry, and even reading signs and omens in the world around you

The real value of divination is in planning and prevention. If you like the answers you receive, continue on. If it looks like trouble ahead, adjust your course of action and see how your new plan affects the outcome. In this way you can use divination to fine tune your future and start living the life you've always dreamed of.

978-0-7387-0384-8, 264 pp., 5³⁄₁₆ x 8 **$14.99**

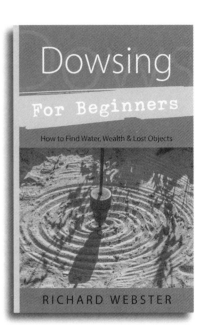

Dowsing

For Beginners

How to Find Water, Wealth & Lost Objects

RICHARD WEBSTER

Dowsing for Beginners
How to Find Water, Wealth & Lost Objects
RICHARD WEBSTER

This book provides everything you need to know to become a successful dowser. Dowsing is the process of using a dowsing rod or pendulum to divine for anything you wish to locate: water, oil, gold, ancient ruins, lost objects or even missing people. Dowsing can also be used to determine if something is safe to eat or drink, or to diagnose and treat allergies and diseases.

Learn about the tools you'll use: angle and divining rods, pendulums, wands-even your own hands and body can be used as dowsing tools! Explore basic and advanced dowsing techniques, beginning with methods for dowsing the terrain for water. Find how to dowse anywhere in the world without leaving your living room, with the technique of map dowsing. Discover the secrets of dowsing to determine optimum planting locations; to monitor your pets' health and well-being; to detect harmful radiation in your environment; to diagnose disease; to determine psychic potential; to locate archeological remains; to gain insight into yourself, and more! *Dowsing for Beginners* is a complete "how-to-do-it" guide to learning an invaluable skill.

978-1-56718-802-8, 240 pp., 5³⁄₁₆ x 8   **$14.99**

To order, call 1-877-NEW-WRLD or visit llewellyn.com
Prices subject to change without notice

Scrying

For Beginners

Use Your Unconscious Mind to
See Beyond the Senses

DONALD TYSON

Scrying for Beginners
Donald Tyson

Scrying for Beginners is for anyone who longs to sit down before the mirror or crystal and lift the rolling grey clouds that obscure their depths. Scrying is a psychological technique to deliberately acquire information by extrasensory means through the unconscious mind. For the first time, all forms of scrying are treated in one easy-to-read, practical book. They include such familiar methods as crystal gazing, pendulums, black mirrors, Ouija™ boards, dowsing rods, aura reading, psychometry, automatic writing and automatic speaking. Also treated are ancient techniques not widely known today, such as Babylonian oil scrying, fire gazing, Egyptian lamp scrying, water scrying, wind scrying, ink scrying, shell-hearing and oracular dreaming.

978-1-56718-746-5, 320 pp., 5³⁄₁₆ x 8   **$16.99**